DESERT TRAVELS

Motorbike Journeys in the Sahara and West Africa

by

Chris Scott

The Travellers' Bookshop
(Bernard J Shapero Rare Books)
32 St. George Street,
London W1R 0EA

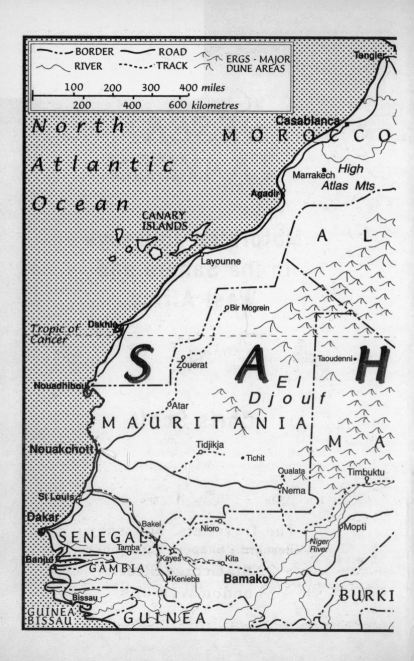

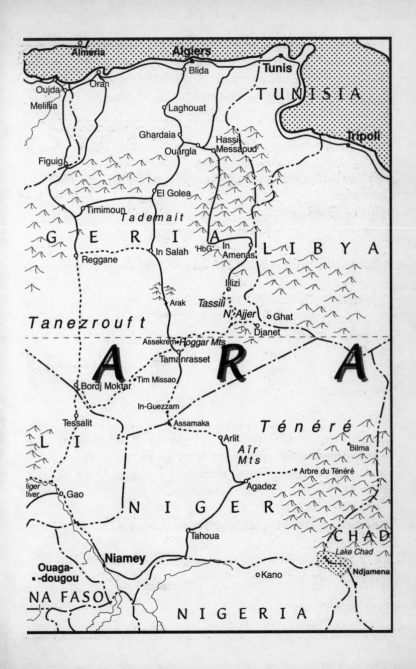

Thanks to Lucy Ridout for editing and ideas, Robert Strauss for ideas and Emmanuelle Betham for help with the French (bad French is written as it was spoken). And thanks also to Lucinda Boyle and the resources of Bernard J. Shapero Rare Books.

Front photo: near Tin-Tarabine, Tassili-Hoggar by Mike Spencer. (Mike, if you ever read this, I owe you some money. CS)
Back cover: Diafarabé on the Niger River by Ian Cartwright.
Maps by Chris Scott.
Cover design with the help of Si Melber.

Printed and bound in Great Britain by The Guernsey Press.

A CIP catalogue record of this book is available from the British Library.

ISBN 1874472 505

THE DESERT

INTO WEST AFRICA

THE DESERT

He had imagined that the Sahara was a mere adventure and that what was essential in life lay in Europe; but he will discover with disgust that it was here in the desert he possessed his veritable treasures – this prestige of the sand, the night, the silence, this homeland of wind and stars.

Wind, Sand and Stars
Antoine de Saint-Exupéry

Tamanrasset and the Fearful Void

Wincing against the pelting rain, I gritted my teeth and accelerated into the darkness, chasing the red glow of Alain's taillight. I shuddered as water started trickling down my neck and out of the sodden sleeves of my jacket. Up ahead something seemed to be driving right at me, headlights blaring. Blinded by the glare, I hit the brakes too hard causing the overloaded bike to wobble alarmingly. I panicked, left side of the road? right side? The lights flared nearer and fearing a head-on collision, I swerved right onto the roadside gravel. The locked front wheel slewed sideways steering the bike into a ditch while I flew over the bars to land with a helmet-cracking thump on the road.
So ended my first day in Africa.

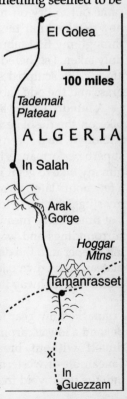

We camped in the mud by the side of the road and next morning, waking stiff and bruised under still leaden skies, Alain shot off south, perhaps seeing me as a liability. Though we'd ignored each other on the boat over to Algiers, we made contact while crossing the Atlas mountains a day later. Swallowing our Lone Biker pride, rode on together into the night – contrary to all advice about driving in

Africa. It had begun to rain as we came over the high plains beyond the mountains but, swept along by Alain's south-bound urgency, I'd tagged along until the unfamiliarity of it all overwhelmed me and I'd crashed.

With Alain gone I loaded up the sorry looking bike, eased on my wet leathers and set off. What the daylight had revealed here, 200 miles south of the coast, was hardly inspiring: a flat drab landscape of shallow ditches and rubble, touched lightly by functional man-made installations and roadside wrecks. I droned down past Laghouat hoping that with every southbound mile the temperature would rise and the desert scenery bloom. Sure enough the sun came out to dry off my clothes and just north of El Golea, now well within the Sahara's northern perimeter, I rode through my first fabulous nest of roadside dunes. Pictures duly taken, I slithered down the bank and wandered in awe among the sculpted sands mellowed by flecks of slender grass and the odd thorny tree.

A hundred miles later I ran into Alain tinkering with his bike on the desolate Tademait Plateau, south of El Golea. Although he'd been boasting about his hybrid BMW's superb performance, his battery had suddenly died so I lent him my bike to get it recharged back in El Golea. Returning a few hours later, he made a snide (if accurate) comment on my sluggish bike before whizzing off again to make up for lost time. In the meantime I'd had a chance to soak up my surroundings and was starting to feel excited about heading deeper into the desert. I continued across the brooding plateau at my own pace until night fell and drew me off the crumbling highway into a sheltered dip.

I unpacked my gear for my first night alone in the Sahara. Beyond a low escarpment to the west, the true plateau continued without break to merge into the featureless Tanezrouft of western Algeria. As I watched the sun sink into the twilit void from the crest of the escarpment, a mesmerising quality overcame me, like that fatal magnetism experienced at a cliff edge. The emptiness to either side of the road seemed to represent insanity, oblivion, the darkness beyond reason. To stray away from this lifeline would lead ultimately to death.

Out here alone, lacking society's tendency towards rationality, anything could happen. Nothing existed to which I could anchor my reason except my own questioning consciousness and my bike.

I tried walking away from the bike and immediately sensed the tension of an imaginary elastic cord drawing me back to the machine and the security of the known world it represented. Mental disorientation and panic seemed just a breath away and I found myself constantly looking back over my tracks towards the bike in case it disappeared. The urge towards the unknown fascinated me, yet the compulsion towards the familiar held me back. Experimenting further with this new sensation, I tried running into the emptiness but the current of prudence proved too strong.

As a cocky noviciate, the desert was indeed a place of fear that night, its implicit menace teasing at my most elemental anxieties. Yet my next camp in the Arak Gorge had all the homely coziness of a cowboy's cactus camp and playing at scaring myself in the desert is not something I've bothered repeating.

My reasons for being here at all were fairly ordinary: an adventurous twenty one-year-old setting off to explore one small part of the world, oblivious to the hardships which eventually dampen our wanderlust. Bob, a fellow despatch rider, had expressed his intention to ride back to the Kenya of his birth. I'd suggested accompanying him across the Sahara where I'd split west for the Ivory Coast, mainly because it sounded nice and African. Though Bob's resolve soon waned, I became captivated with the opportunity for motorbike adventure. I'd work my passage across the Med, cross the desert via an interesting route and, if need be, sell my camera in the Ivory Coast (such luxury items doubtless fetching a fortune there) before shipping myself back. Or I'd carry on. Many other travellers I've met admit to similar precocious adventures: hitchhiking to India with grape-picked savings, cycling to Dakar the hard way. At that age optimism, enthusiasm and curiosity are the fuel of your fantasies, limited only by a flat wallet or fear.

Woken into utter despair again by the loathsome patter of drizzle – in future years something bad or weird would always happen to me on the sinister Tademait – I caught up with Alain yet again, broken down on the outskirts of In Salah. After the previous evening's haste he was now all too keen for us to ride together across the desert all the way to the Ivory Coast, his home. I waited for him to get fixed up in In Salah but soon decided that, old desert hand though he was, I really didn't like Alain and so I slipped away south towards Tamanrasset (Tam for short), negotiating my way along a road which, though only recently laid, was already in tatters.

That year in the early Eighties the winter rains had been unusually heavy, wreaking havoc not only with the roads, but also with the road-users – myself included. Two hundred miles down the route at the Arak Gorge a flash flood had completely washed away several miles of road. All that remained were undermined ledges of thick tar mantle which hung like cornices over fresh deposits of powdery sand. And down near Tamanrasset the rains had carved a 100ft-wide chasm right through the road, a gap so wide that it looked like a bridge was about to be built across it.

It's said there was just one year when you could theoretically drive the 1200 miles from Algiers to Tam in two very long days. Since that time the combination of freight trucks, extreme summer temperatures and rare but destructive storms have periodically ruined the metalled road, rendering it unusable for hundreds of miles at a stretch. For years the Algerian Army has been pressed into the

Sisyphusian task of incrementally extending the trans-Saharan Highway southwards, but the plan to link the Algerian section with the paved road that runs up from Niger seems doomed, as newly laid sections crumble in the road builders' wake and civil unrest makes more pressing claims on army personnel.

But I was experiencing other problems. Quite apart from the demoralising crash and my subsequent aches, the dreary desert was failing to match up to my expectations. Although I knew that the Sahara wasn't all just three million square miles of rosy sand dunes and fluttering palms, did it have to be so cold, wet, expensive and boring? South of Arak at least the topography had become more varied, but the short detours off-road had also exposed the fact that my overloaded XT500 handled like a wheelbarrow. Once I got to Tam something would have to be done.

Situated in what is just about the exact geographical centre of the Sahara, Tamanrasset was during the Eighties *the* focal point for all Saharan travellers. Pretty much anyone making their way across the Sahara or into the Hoggar mountains was obliged to pass through the outpost and, in the relative coolness of the winter months, the dusty streets of this otherwise uninteresting frontier town would be alive with the barter and gossip of tourists, traders and local merchants.* Fittingly for its epicentral position, Tam lacks adequate reserves of water, which is rationed to just two hours at each end of the day. Its isolation hardly makes it an ideal place to live; goods are expensive, summers desperately hot and communications poor. Tam is nothing more than a bloated entrepôt, a place to weld a chassis, visit the Hoggar, cross-examine other travellers and move on.

---

* Political strife has since put a damper on recreational desert manoeuvres and the Tam of the late 1990s must seem like a ghost town, with the Algerian civil war making access from the north almost impossible and the Tuareg insurgents rendering the southern approach too dangerous for casual visitors.

Not surprisingly, the people of Tamanrasset seem rather a disaffected lot: many of them were originally drawn here by the prospect of the tourist dollar, but are now (or were then) inevitably wearied by the constant flow of intrepid tourists. In contrast, the indigenous Ahaggar Tuareg cut striking figures. The sight of these tall, proud nomads (*Ahaggar* means "the proud") strolling down the street, their white *taguelmoust* (veil) pushed up to a narrow eye slit and their voluminous indigo *gandoura* (robe) billowing out, is my most enduring memory of the town. Vain to a degree you wouldn't necessarily associate with nomads in a mirrorless land, they know their appearance alone inspires admiration, not to mention their recently revived reputation as desert bandits.

Unencumbered by property these mysterious and romanticised men blow in and out of town to trade or take work as drivers or desert guides, rarely lingering for more than a few days before returning to their families in the villages of the nearby Hoggar mountains. Also known as the Hoggar Tuareg, this was the fiercest of the Tuareg clans who thwarted French expansion into the Sahara before being finally defeated in 1907. Since Algeria's independence in 1962, the distant government has shown the customary hostility towards its nomadic citizens, suppressing their indifference towards unseen national borders and meaningless permits. Persistent droughts have further undermined the Tuareg (singular "Targui") way of life and decimated the camel herds where their wealth traditionally lay. Their's is the sad but common story of a pessimistic Vanishing Peoples TV documentary. Age-old cultures and traditions wiped away in the face of the advancing modern age.

After a couple of days in town during which time I'd sent some junk home and modified the bike, I'd been gratified to encounter other bikers returning from far more extensive and equally ill-equipped travels. Then one day, as ready as

I was ever likely to be, I filled up with enough fuel to get me to the Algerian border post at In Guezzam and blithely headed south to the end of the unfinished road.

In setting out to ride across the sands, I felt I was being drawn into a black hole in the certainty that what was humanly possible must also be humanly survivable. I was going alone only because I didn't foresee any difficulties during the crossing, thinking I merely had to keep going south until I got to the other side. I'd no idea what to expect from the dreaded *piste* (as tracks are known hereabouts) except for the endlessly re-read description from the *Sahara Handbook*. This promised an unmarked stretch of around 400 miles: 250 miles south to Assamaka, the Niger frontier post set on a hill of powdery soft sand and then southeast-ish for another 150-odd miles to Arlit where the sealed road resumed.

As I rode along a smooth section of built-up track ready to receive its coating of tarmac, an armed soldier flagged me down and attempted to extort my collection of pornography, cigarettes and whisky. Lacking all these items I instead offered him some sickly Algerian sweets which I was myself munching with such nervous ardour that I eventually pulled out a filling. Scoffing at my infantile trib-ute, he gruffly sent me on my way.

All too soon the embryonic road came to an end and a mass of parallel and corrugated tracks fanned out along the Oued Tin Amzi, winding their own way south (a *oued*, or *wadi* in the eastern Sahara, is a dry river bed). This was it, the bouncy end of the springboard. By picking the clearest tracks and following them for 200 miles or so I should come to the first landmark, the Laouni dunes and a ruined fort where the pistes would converge past a distant escarpment and lead me down to In Guezzam. Even today the Michelin "953 – Africa; North and West" map describes this route as a *piste peu balisée* , and as I soon found out, the *balises* (posts marked with "TAM 135" or "I-GN 265") were so infrequent as to be useless. There were no landmarks or signs of any

kind, just tracks, some faint, others deep, but all continual-
ly and perplexingly expiring and recommencing somewhere else, demanding a constant eye on their orientation.
Though it seemed highly improbable to ride for 200 miles
across the desert looking for dunes, my nerves calmed as I
slowly got into the merry swing of riding over the desert
floor. I soon learned to avoid lighter patches of sand which
were dangerously soft, sucking the power away from my
wheels and forcing me to rev the engine hard to keep moving.

After a couple of hours I felt secure enough to stop at one
of the scarce balises for a photo. Up till then the very
thought of stopping in the panoramic desolation had filled
me with trepidation, as if just by temporarily ceasing
motion I would succumb to the overpowering force of the
desert. Now I allowed myself some guarded excitement
about what lay ahead, but as I settled the camera in the
sand, pressed the shutter and dashed over to the bike to
adopt my rugged pose, I noticed an ominous patch of fuel
spreading on the sand under the bike. Eliminating the likely and repairable causes of loose fuel taps or a blocked car-
burettor, I hurriedly unscrewed the filler cap and peered in,
rocking the bike vigourously from side to side. The desperate motion produced only a faint tinkle of remaining fuel.
The marker post indicated that I'd covered about a third of
the distance to In Guezzam which should have been half a
tank's worth. Now the tank was nearly empty and getting
emptier by the second. This luckless trip which had hardly
got off to a promising start was now about to turn in on me
with big boots and baseball bats.

Up the Creek

My first impulse was to find some shelter, a tall order seeing as I hadn't so much as passed a tree since leaving the oued that morning. Nevertheless, in a state of restrained panic I felt compelled to start the bike and get moving, a rather pointless display of our adrenaline-charged "flight" instinct when faced with danger. It merely delayed the only solution to my problem: finding and repairing the leak.

Within a few minutes I chanced upon one of the many shells of abandoned cars which litter the piste, a green BMW 2002 with every removable component bar its body long since scavenged. The car symbolised a tenuous link with humanity and ultimate safe-ty, and enabled me to regain my composure as I hastily pulled the bike apart. Setting the damaged tank on the car's front wing dis-closed a broken mounting brack-et which had allowed the tank to shake loose over rough ground, ultimately cracking it. The photo stop had been a fortuitous break as carrying on with my fuel drib-bling away unknowingly might have eventually stranded me, unable to get to either In Guezzam or Tamanrasset. And because the piste here was up to ten miles wide there might have been a day or two's wait for a vehicle to pass close enough to

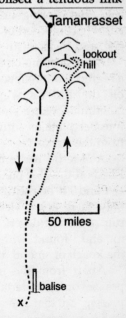

see me; I'd seen no one since leaving the tarmac.

I set to repairing the tank with some Araldite which I'd propitiously swiped as I walked out the front door of my mother's house a few weeks earlier. Now that I knew what was wrong I didn't consider I was in serious danger; I had enough water to last up to a week and at the very worst I could burn a tyre to make a smoky signal.

Within an hour a truck passed by a mile or so away, crunching its gears agonisingly over the irregular piste. I began walking towards it, waving as I went, certain that it would stop as all other vehicles had done without being prompted on the Highway up north. But, either oblivious or unbothered by my obvious distress, this truck ground on southwards to the border. As the sun set and the glue hardened I thought carefully about what I should do: carry on with my still overloaded and now unreliable bike or call it a day and head back the 150-odd kilometres to Tam? I decided on the latter. I'd seen enough both of the dreary, cold, flat, boring desert and of Algeria (which seemed entirely composed of cheerless young men in bomber jackets), and I was unsure which was more miserable.

After sleeping on a sandy bed beside the car, I scrawled a regretful but relieved epitaph to my solo Saharan venture on the BMW's wing next morning, collected a few Neolithic-looking stone tools and the car's chassis serial number plate as souvenirs and tentatively filled the tank from the jerrican.

As I left, I had a notion that the repair, which had finished off the glue on the final successful attempt, might not last and I'd be racing the leaking fuel back to Tam. It was only then, acknowledging that I was effectively "on the run" from the desert, that my fears finally caught up with me and I found, without really knowing why, that I'd lost the knack of smooth riding I'd refined the day before.

Apart from the mind games of that first night, the praiseworthy undertaking of Conquering My Fear was not present on that first Saharan agenda, nor has it figured since. Like anyone developing a skill, in later trips I enjoyed cautiously extending the boundaries of my experience. But with this knowledge of deserty things came also the knowledge of fear. Fear in the Sahara is not the sudden shock of a near miss, it is the constant nagging awareness of the consequences of something going wrong and of your utter helplessness in the face of that event. Fear of the many ways in which things had gone wrong before and how they could go wrong and stay wrong again. In coming years I learned to detest that momentary panic clawing in the chest at even the most minor error when riding a bike alone in the desert. But I've also found that fear is a useful possession; one that I've recognised as I neared my limits while enjoying my Saharan explorations Nothing is conquered except ignorance.

Geoffrey Moorhouse describes reaching similar enlightenment the hard way in *The Fearful Void*, his attempt to walk the width of the Sahara alone, in the early Seventies. With a recklessness that must have had his publisher drooling with delight, he stated that his trek – presumably the most dangerous thing he could think of at the time – was an attempt to

> examine the bases of my fear, to observe in the closest possible proximity how a human being copes with his most fundamental funk.

In his words, fear was "the most corrosive element attacking the goodness of the human spirit" and perhaps here Moorhouse's and my understanding of the F-word differs: to me it's not an emotion which cripples humanity, but a useful instinct which enables long life and prosperity.

Barring physical fitness, Moorhouse boasted of his complete lack of experience for this unprecedented feat: the self-deprecating "Adventures of Greenhorn" ploy of so many contemporary travelogues since Eric Newby's likeable short escapade in the Hindu Kush. Not surprisingly, after great personal suffering Moorhouse's absurd stunt ended prematurely in Tamanrasset, about a third of the way through. He'd learned what most people spotted after one viewing of *Lawrence of Arabia*, that the desert does not suffer fools and that the biggest void was in his vast lack of experience and understanding. That, and the appaling way the intolerant hero treated his desert guides makes it hard to admire his achievement.[*]

There's a subtle but significant difficulty when riding northwards on a piste in the northern hemisphere when the sun is generally behind you; it's hard to explain but here goes. Imagine you're crossing a road with the sun in your face casting a black band of shadow underneath the kerb ahead. Even if everything around you is the same hue, you'd still spot the shadowy lip of the kerb and adjust your step accordingly as you approach it. Try this in the opposite direction with the sun *behind* you, and you'll find the glare much greater, with no helpful shadows highlighting the relief of the ground or the step of the kerb ahead of you. Before you know it you trip over and go sprawling.

So it is when heading south in the Sahara; the sun is generally high and in your face, highlighting a host of tiny but informative shadows and shades of the terrain ahead, most especially defining the lips of sharp-edged ridges which you can then ride round.

Heading north I couldn't work out why everything was so bright and why it was so hard to ride smoothly after yesterday's valuable lesson. Are some days brighter than others in the Sahara? After a few near misses I hit an unseen foot-high creek bank and went over the bars. Fortunately everything breakable on the bike was already broken so damage was negligible, but the harmless spill unnerved

---

[*] Then again, it's possible that his trip's unexpected failure led to the contrivance of the "exploration of my fears" angle to pad out an otherwise inconclusive book. The Sahara was eventually traversed from the Atlantic to the Red Sea a decade or so later by the experienced cameleer Michael Asher and his wife Mariantonietta Peru. Their gruelling trek is described in Asher's book, *The Impossible Journey*.

me. Checking the repaired tank for renewed leaks, I forced myself to slow down, watch where I was riding and take it easy.

After an hour I spotted a balise declaring "95km" to Tamanrasset, just a couple of hours at this pace and well within my remaining fuel reserves. With this comforting information I rewarded myself with a rest stop and clambered onto a rocky outcrop – only to be pestered by a swarm of flies. At least that meant that human habitation was near.

Another hour and I found myself riding into the arms of a forming river bed and with relief anticipated army camps and the frayed end of the Highway leading swiftly to Tamanrasset. I assumed it was the Oued Tin Amzi, down which I'd ridden only yesterday when Agadez and the palm-fringed beaches of the Ivory Coast had been my destination. That was all behind me now: retreat had set resolutely in my mind and a speedy, trouble-free return home was all I was interested in. I had happily accepted the defeat of my plan which had sounded like an exciting adventure, but which I'd never really expected to succeed. "Agadez sounded so nice too" I'd written with some regret on the side of the sheltering wreck that morning. It was another five years before I was to find this out for myself when a no less drama-packed crossing finally delivered me to the south side of the Sahara.

The low fringe of the Hoggar was now rising on the horizon. Any minute now, I thought, The Road, Deliverance, and a fast run home. Alas, eager not to overshoot Tamanrasset and ride off into the oblivion west of town, I had in fact overcompensated by unconsciously riding too far to the east. (These were all relative observations gleaned from the sun's shadow: the precision of a compass is only useful when you know where you are or can identify a given landmark marked on a map.) I knew nothing more than that Tam was north and that's were I wanted to be.

The creek narrowed and turned west and even south and so I crested the rubble hills which bordered it in the vain hope that the adjacent valley would unveil the glistening black tar surface which I was surely close to by now. No such luck. Struggling up another trackless sandy stream bed, I saw still more signals that civilisation was just around the corner: a grazing donkey and even an army jeep which whizzed by without stopping. North at all costs was my motto, any which way as long as it was north. And so I found myself battling through the soft sand and rocks of an unlikely creek bed littered with thorny acacia branches which within minutes flattened my rear tyre.

As I now know, it's not uncommon to perish a ridiculously short distance from safety: if you're on your last legs – which I was not – any distance can be just too far to manage. So it is that bodies are found just a dune's width from the vital well that would have saved them. Still, all such morbidity was far from my mind as I removed the wheel and picked the thorns from the tyre. In the warmth of winter my situation was hardly life-threatening; the worst I might have to do was to keep riding the bike on a flat tyre (something I ended up doing on *both* wheels a few years later) until I got to Tam. The tyre and even the wheel might be ruined but, like a nomad and his camel, I've always considered my bikes to be ultimately expendable if engaged in the service of getting me out of trouble.

I didn't know where I was except that I was surely somewhere close to Tamanrasset. The road had to be nearby but just exactly where I could only guess. Being close to some known point but temporarily lost tends to weigh uncomfortably on the mind. It's often impossible to relax let alone sleep in such a situation, and so I decided to scramble up a nearby hill before dealing with the puncture. Perhaps I could ease my mind with some good news: a landmark, a radio tower maybe, or even the longed-for road winding along a neighbouring valley.

Reaching the summit I looked around to the west where,

if my easterly drift proved correct, deliverance surely lay. At first I saw nothing, just more of the low, burnt orange hills into which I'd wandered and which I distinctly recalled passing through the day before. Then a couple of miles away I thought I spotted the olive tents of an army camp, doubtless housing the crew that were building the road. Delighted with finding just the sort of sign I'd sought, I memorised its position in the maze of creeks and clambered back down to the bike. I took my time with the puncture, eager not to pinch a tube and ruin the whole operation, and when it was done I cautiously put all my gear together and set off up the labyrinthine oueds to salvation.

I never found the army camp which had governed my decision, and it would be tempting to say I saw a benign mirage which guided me back to safety. Expecting to see the tents and jeeps, and doubtless some kind of hostile alarm at my approach, I instead stumbled across a tarmac road. For a moment I thought it could not be *the* road: perhaps it was some classified by-pass leading to a secret nerve-gas compound? I certainly didn't recognise the area which I'd ridden through thirty hours earlier. In the end I came to my senses: there was only one road for hundreds of miles and this was part of it. I picked what I thought to be the more northerly direction and found myself back in Tamanrasset within half an hour.

On the Run

Having set my mind on retreat, I now *could not wait* to be rid of the desert's cloying grasp. Leaving Tam the next day I rode north, indifferent to my surroundings and fixed only with a single-minded fervour to wind up this foolhardy escapade as swiftly as possible. Further thorn punctures pricked at my resolve, and one afternoon in my haste I took a westward gamble towards Timimoun, rather than detouring 80 miles to El Golea for fuel. Another few degrees of the Earth's latitude and tomorrow night I'd be in Morocco: virtually Europe and soon, home.

The sun sank before me as I sagged closer and closer to the tank in spine-creaking exhaustion, emerging in the zonked-out, engine-humming trance that a prolonged day's ride induces. At times I greedily ticked away the marker posts which drew me to Timimoun in ten-kilometre increments, or anxiously re-calculated fuel consumption figures while pressing myself into a

lightweight ornament of aerodynamic efficiency. At one point a roadhouse promised the hope of petrol pumps, but the site was deserted and I cursed the fuel wasted in slowing down and accelerating again. An hour after sunset, as the moon began to rise over my back, the engine spluttered and died just 14 miles from Timimoun. Low on dinars and with vital permits nearing their "renew-by" date, yet again my frantic retreat had been thwarted.

I drained my petrol stove into the tank and gained another mile or two. Then I tried pushing the bike, but the slightest uphill gradient repulsed the heavy machine. Parking by the roadside, I decided to wait for a passing car, jerrican in hand. In the clear desert night lights can be seen over 20 miles away, and I watched avidly as a pair of headlights dipped and bobbed across the landscape for more than half an hour. The vehicle approached, headlights blazing and I stood up waving the can with fairly obvious intent. To my amazement it flew by.

Just as when the truck had grumbled past my stricken bike at the green BMW, there was no help when it was needed, but surely here on the road someone must eventually stop. Like an overdue commuter at a bus stop, I glared fixedly down the moonlit highway waiting for a reprieve. Nothing came for an hour until again a pair of intermittent, ever-brightening lights loomed closer from the east. Again I swung my jerrican meaningfully into the dazzling beams. This time the car slowed down and stopped.

A splash of siphoned fuel was all I needed, but the van's two occupants had other ideas and insisted on giving me a lift to nearby Timimoun where they assured me I could buy all the fuel I wanted. Something about my benefactors gave me the creeps, especially when they insisted I sit between them on the bench seat. As we drove along slowly into the night they asked if I was hungry and offered me a crust of bread which I accepted and gnawed on politely. Then they started talking money.

'How much will you give us to drive you to Timimoun?'

'Nothing I'm afraid, I have very little money left.'

'But you must pay us something, the desert is danger-ous, you can't expect a ride for free,' said the passenger menacingly.

Trapped between the two of them I was now convinced that the sinister desert and everyone in it were slowly drag-ging me back into its black heart. I eyed-up the gear stick, calculating how to jam it into reverse before fighting my way out of the skidding car – an improbable fantasy that's crossed most hitchhikers' minds.

'Okay I can give you fifty dinars,' I proposed.

'Fifty dinars? This is not enough. You must give us five hundred.'

'Fifty dinars is plenty and it's all I have.' I said, experi-menting with some bluff defiance. The talk stopped for a while as I urged the lights of Timimoun to silhouette the oncoming hill. Soon, some wire-fenced compounds appeared and presently the opaque gloaming of street lighting.

'Give me the fifty dinars,' demanded the passenger, knowing that the trip would soon be over.

I fished out the note which I'd stuffed in a pocket away from my remaining cash and handed it over as we drove down into the town.

'Do you want us to drive you back to your bike?'

Knowing that this meant more money, I declined the offer.

'Ah, but a bike is not safe in the desert, it will be stolen in the night.'

I shrugged my shoulders, feigning indifference at their thinly-veiled threat. It would be a shame to lose the bike, but I had my money, films and passport – they could do what they wanted with the bike, it was crap anyway. They let me out at the petrol station and I watched them drive off to the far end of town – they didn't turn back. It had been a long day, most of it on broken roads, and now with a full can of fuel and little chance of a lift back into the desert that night, I relaxed and let the weariness seep through me. Walking over to some roadside dunes I settled among them, using the jerrican as a pillow, and fell quickly asleep.

Next morning I stood up, brushed-off the sand and was ready for the day. Slithering back down to the road I began walking into the desert, hoisting the heavy container on my shoulder. Fourteen miles – at the very worst it would take me five hours of walking. I tried hitching but the two or three cars rushed straight by. My hatred for the place tightened and with it my stubborn resolution to get out and never come back. At an edge-of-town building site a lorry was heading out in my direction and, abandoning my usual temerity, I boldly asked for a lift. The elderly driver wasn't having it, explaining that he wasn't going far, but I insisted that my bike was only half an hour down the road and that even a short distance would do, and so reluctantly he let me in.

In fact he *was* only going a short distance, on the lookout for a handy pile of sand for the building site. A lorry looking for sand in the Sahara – how absurd! As we drove into the desert I watched him eyeing up likely dunelettes while I silently urged no, keep going, there's some lovely top-grade builders' sand just past my bike, honest. But even as I thought this, and after just a few short minutes in the cab, he set his heart on his dream dune and letting me out, drove off to scoop it up.

Half a mile further on down the road and my determination started to wilt. Striding along in full riding gear, with twenty litres of fuel on my shoulder (why twenty when three would have done? don't ask…) and no water to quench my thirst, it was now impossible to compete with the nagging heat. I sat down on the can, breathless and dry mouthed, marching on only when I saw a car coming so as to give an impression of dynamic intent worthy of sympathy. But no one stopped.

Finally, with a well overdue reversal of ill-fortune, a pristine Land Cruiser came gliding to a halt and I was ushered into the back by the smiling face of Sheikh Bou Ahmadi. A brief chat in perfect English disclosed that I was from London. Oh how he *loved* London, what a great city! As we spoke, his taciturn chauffeur sped us along at ninety miles an hour and within a few minutes the outline of my bike appeared by the roadside. With my best wishes and avowed thanks, the Sheikh disappeared in an air-conditioned dash towards El Golea.

I left Algeria at the desert border town of Figuig where a pair of penniless German boys sat on their impounded Capri, waiting for money from home. Like them, I had to leave my vehicle at the customs post and take a day's bus ride to the northern town of Oujda to buy insurance. Another delay, but at least Algeria was behind me now. My mood began to lighten and I bantered lightheartedly with the hotel keeper in Figuig for his *djellaba* which I thought would make a pleasingly gothic dressing gown.

Back in Oujda later that week, on my safely insured bike, young boys on mopeds swerved into me in an effort to sell me dope or Algerian dinars. After what already seemed like the unpopulated solace of the desert, I found the repetitive attentions of countless Moroccan hustlers utterly maddening, but a day or so later I swung my legs happily from a portside ramp in the Spanish enclave of Melillia. Tomorrow the morning boat would deliver me to the recognisable civilisation of Europe. I was rather pleased with myself for, though I couldn't distinguish hash from a stale fruit cake, I'd bought a few bundles of likely-looking green powder for my potheaded chums back home. Whatever it was, it only cost 50p a bag and who knows, if it was the wicked "Double Zero" numerous pushers had been trying to foist on me, I might even make a little money.

As I sat by the docks, relieved that the end was in sight, a dark figure wrapped like a monk in his hooded djellaba emerged from the gloom and approached me.

'*Bonsoir,*' he said.

"*Soir,*' I offered warily.

'*Anglais, eh?*'

'*Oui.*'

'You go to Almeria tomorrow, yes?'

'Uh hm.'

'You want to make some money, *hashish*?'

Smugly assured that I'd already scored my prize stash for just 50p a bag, I declined his offer. Inevitably, he persisted.

'A kilo only 30,000 dirhams.'

Hmmm, on a kilo I could definitely make some money, and presuming that I was technically in Spain there would be no more Customs checks, but I asked him anyway.

'No, no. Tomorrow you drive straight on to the boat and at Almeria you drive off. You are already in Spain, there are no Customs.'

I didn't have 30,000 dirhams, but I was sure that could be negotiated, and the idea of making a few hundred illicit pounds excited me. I could stash the brick on the bike, maybe *under the seat* where they'd never think of looking, and I'd be home free, trip paid for. Whatever wisdom I'd mustered by turning back at the green BMW or climbing that Lookout Hill, I'd clearly squandered in the intervening 1500 miles. I agreed to look at the deal and talk money. The dark figure disappeared back into the night and, luckily for me, never returned.

Next morning, before I'd even boarded the boat, Customs officials were busy withdrawing probes from my seat and sniffing them, peering into the tank with fibre optic scanners and tapping furtive cavities. Keeping my cool while my insides spun like a blender, the bags of killer weed stashed in a little tool box managed to escape their search, but on arriving in Almeria they really put the works on. On the quay a row of Alsatian sniffers with MAs in drug retrieval descended methodically on the disembarkees and their luggage. Having recently seen *Midnight*

Express, my one thought was relief that I was about to be locked in a Spanish jail for a year or two and not a vile Moroccan one.

The clever dog sniffed around me and my bike, responding obediently to the commands of its master. Oh God, he's close to the tool box, any minute now it'll be That Scene: the officer will stand back and with a signal, a score of machine guns will lock onto me. My arms will shoot up in defeat while bodily fluids dribbled over my boot tops. Spanish jail. Tabloids. Humiliation.

As it happened the canny sniffers weren't all they were cracked up to be and I left the docks with Bruno, a Quebequoise hippie I'd met on the boat. Nearly broke himself, he knew of a beachside cave where we could stay until some money came through. During that week he broke in his Moroccan *tam-tams* while confidently predicting Quebec's independence within six months. I'd never encountered a genuine hippie before and marvelled at his Stoned Humour and traveller's guile. He embellished the cave with a washed-up fridge door – how nutty! – and showed me how to save fuel by letting part-cooked food stew in a knotted plastic bag. Having just emerged from a mammoth two-month session in Morocco he bragged about a yacht-bound girlfriend on the Riviera and another lover in Paris who would be sending him funds.

My money came through and I left Bruno with a loan which he promised to send back from Quebec along with some Maple Sauce. Never trust a hippie I've since been told... I rode up through Spain, taking advantage of the helmet-free laws at that time and the surprising profusion of deserted buildings to sleep in. Ferry strikes in Santander prolonged the journey across the interminable fir plantations of Bordeaux to freezing, fogbound Brittany. Sat snugly gratified on the twilit deck of a Portsmouth-bound ferry, I recall relaying my Saharan skirmish to some spellbound school kids who'd spotted me on my bike in St Malo.

When I got home I gave the stash away. They told me it

was *kif*, a mildly narcotic snuff snorted by old men and worth around 50p. Someone rolled some up anyway and gave themselves a bad headache. I knew the feeling, but one thing was certain, I was never going anywhere near the Sahara ever again.

Trip of a Lifetime

Seven years later I was planning my fifth visit to the Sahara. It had taken about eighteen months for the miseries of that demoralising baptism to metamorphose into pearlescent memories. Why this should happen is mystifying; in my case it must have been the victory of rose-tinted optimism over miserable experience.

But by now I'd become aware of the limitations of solo bike travels in the desert, a fact that everyone who *didn't* undertake this activity instinctively knew. Any route longer than the most straightforward two to three day pistes of around 400 miles demanded a payload that a bike and its rider could barely manage, and this allowed very little margin for error. What's more it was often first-time riders struggling in the elements with their ungainly machines who came to grief.

So, responding to the supposed demand of "soft adventure" tourism, I figured there must be a score of bike-owning punters out there who'd gladly pay to experience the glories of the Sahara with the security of an organised tour led by a back-up vehicle. (Thanks to the sensational antics of the Paris-Dakar Rally the Sahara was becoming a well known setting for adventurous biking.) Furthermore it would give me a chance to explore with them and be paid for it! I called my enterprise *Sahara Motorcycle Tours* (SMT), a costly if well-intended fiasco which I would never dare repeat.

As the idea took shape I busied myself with calculators and maps, weaving thrilling itineraries through the deep Algerian Sahara. I agonised for months over what sort of 4WD support vehicle to buy and how to equip it while devising what I thought was a seductive advert for the motorbike press:

OWN A BIG TRAIL BIKE?
Experience of a Lifetime
Three week expedition to
the Algerian Sahara
with 4WD support vehicle
Four places only, £1099

I looked with pride as the ads appeared in a few carefully selected bike publications, read avidly by readers with the right mixture of disposable income, soft adventurousness and free time. And *only* four places – stand back: the phone was about to blow off the wall!

But nothing happened. Not only nothing, but *absolutely* nothing, not even time-wasting enquiries or requests for brochures from which the travel industry estimates a 5% success rate. But it was a Trip of a Lifetime. Hadn't they heard of the shimmering dunes, the excellent weather, the spirit of adventure? Even today I'm still amazed at the lack of response. Eventually Len from Waterloo called up, a young despatcher with the right bike, and Bernie from Guernsey who had a dirt bike too. Len was keen:

'All I gotta do is sell the GSX-R, rebore the Dommie an'

pay back me mum.'

Bernie sounded less sure, but his dad was impressed with my typed information sheet, wrongly thinking I had a computer and was therefore, eminently trustworthy.

Most enquiries came directly from fellow despatch riders; high-earning, motivated and restless individuals eager to get away from the infernal city. Terry, a bright, smartly dressed and self-assured braggart was interested and the Riders' Room where we sporadically met was a repository of festering wellies, not enough ash trays and stagnating coffee cups. Tea bags dried on the walls where they'd been flicked by stress-addled riders and a sign, as yet unabused, explained plainly "No Signature – No Pay". Four-Zero, an affable if slow-witted rider, sat perplexed by the loss of his "between jobs" slippers – he'd yet to notice they'd been nailed to the ceiling by a prankster.

Terry had a suitable bike (in fact like many despatchers, he had several, but only one actually worked) and when we'd cross paths he'd grill me to find a chink in my plans, because Tel was nobody's fool but his own.

'So what support vehicle you takin', then?' he asked.

'Dunno yet, probably an LWB Land Rover with a big diesel.'

'My mate's got a V8 One-Ten Country, I tell you what, it fuckin' shifts that thing!'

'Yeah well a V8's nice but too juicy, it's gotta be a big diesel coz it's safer, simpler, and diesel is dead cheap in Algeria with black market currency.' The idea of dealing with the black market excited him, but he continued:

'What if it breaks down?'

'We'll fix it – it won't break down.' I quickly added in bluff. 'Anyway, there'll be four bikes to tow it to the nearest town, if necessary' I explained, wondering if my improvisation impressed him – I visualised four bikes harnessed like chariot horses to the creaking front bumper while their back wheels spun roosts of sand at the windscreen.

As the weeks rolled on, Terry explained how he'd sent

off to California for a special shock absorber and to Italy for a racing tank, none of which he really needed but, like many bikers, he was in love with the idea of a purposeful racing machine and took to wearing dirt biking gear at work to prove his intentions.

'Whadja reckon about those Michelin Desert tyres, they're fuckin' expensive.' he said with relish. Terry was also a motorbiking epicure, he desired the best of everything and if it was the dearest then so much the better.

'They're good, definitely worth it. They'll last the whole trip and you won't get any punctures. I can get them cheap from Michelin.'

He liked that too, insider dealing, special contacts.

Like a lot of us urban street fighters (as we despatchers preferred to be known) Tel had a bit of an SAS streak in him that he expressed at weekend paintball tournaments. A few other riders also attended these asinine *faux* wars, filling Monday mornings with testaments of their commando-like prowess and multiple deaths. He asked me about the need for weapons out there, should he carry a knife, a paintball dispenser?

'You don't need anything like that' I said, laughing off the idea. 'We'll be camping out in the desert miles from anyone.' I secretly remembered a natty flick knife I'd eventually given away to a helpful trucker on my last trip. The xenophobe in Terry could hold back no longer.

'I'll be carrying a ten-inch blade and if any fuckin' Ayrab comes near me, I'll cut 'is fuckin' bollocks off!' My eyebrows rose and I nodded slowly, groaning inwardly about sharing the Sahara with "Eight-Four, Tel'". Luckily for me he crashed out that summer, got off with one of the reps and bought himself another bike.

One or two other friends of despatching friends got in touch about the big trip. Luca, a young Italian doing a bit of couriering in London, came over one night, but really only wanted a second opinion about the utility of his bike's front disc brake protector. I petitioned Pete, with whom I'd travelled the previous year and whose untimely misfortune after months of planning helped push SMT towards the crucial headed note paper stage. He liked the idea; a chance to safely explore the desert he'd ridden to the brink of, before his wheels had collapsed in terror. Luca begat Mark, a keen young despatcher with his head screwed on. He in turn knew Mike who brought along his temperamentality, wit and exhibitionism. He reminded me of Oliver Reed without the booze. Bob turned up via some mutual connection too. At forty, the oldest in the group, Bob's space ship had left earth in the early Seventies. Although he lacked the alertness and vigour of the others, I liked his drifting ease. That he played in a jazz band called the Mellow Tones summed him up nicely. To Bob the desert was a hubbly-bubbly of romance, not a race track or obstacle course. He hoped we'd get a chance to visit the tiny oasis of Iherir, lost like El Dorado in a valley in the Tassili plateau.

These early recruits soon saw the wisdom of their ways and coughed up handy deposits about which I felt vaguely guilty. Nevertheless the trip was on and so I offered a friend, Clive, a free trip as co-driver and cook. He turned out to be a real asset: both an imaginative cook (a morale-recharging duty not to be undervalued) and a great entertainer, deflecting attention from myself, the aloof and preoccupied Skipper.

Now that I knew the size of the group I could focus on the all important support vehicle. After scouring four-wheel drive magazines for months I settled on something called a Land Rover 101, a Tonka-like wheeled pallet riveted to a cab bristling with cranium-stabbing bracketry and unreachable levers. Land Rover had produced them for the army in the mid-Seventies and now they were being released to the public. Know-all off-roaders rated the 101 highly, a functional all-terrain load carrier embodying that company's once famous disregard for operator comfort and aerodynamics.

A father and son hillbilly engineering outfit in east London fitted my selected shell with a big Ford diesel engine – chosen more because it slotted neatly into the available space than for its suitability. Only months after I returned from the trip did Pete send me a clipping which described the engine in horribly familiar terms: "The six cylinder York engine is not really worth fitting to a Land Rover as it is a heavy, long engine and has many built-in problems, poor starting from cold being the most significant." Although I didn't know it then, I couldn't have said it better myself.

My regular newsletters informed the team of this momentous acquisition and one Saturday morning we all met up on the Ridgeway in Berkshire to ride off-road together, take pictures for a press release and engender what every expedition surely relied on, the gelling of its personnel. Quite how one gels people I didn't really know, something to do with overcoming challenges with shared solutions and holding hands in the dark while swapping names. To be honest it didn't really matter, they were paying me to organise their holiday in the desert, I just had to say when.

As the big day approached we met in a pub I knew in Kings Cross. In the meeting room round the back I'd once listened in on meetings of the "Pentonville Sub Aqua Club", the cunning *nom de guerre* of the London branch of the revolutionary anarchist outfit, Class War. Here they'd spend Sunday evenings arguing about who had room to store the organisation's newspaper or stake out some fascist book shop in the East End.

In the pub Clive, myself and the five clients pored over the final details of our departure, filled out travel and medical insurance forms (which I privately thought to be worthless) and then went back to my place to see a slide show of my last trip. If anyone was in the slightest bit excited, they certainly weren't showing it. With the exception of Pete, they may not have known what to expect, but I certainly did.

And one thing I had was deep misgivings about the whole idea of leading a bunch of bikers into the desert, mollified by the presence of an experienced organiser in an all-terrain support-vehicle. Their experience would be quite different from mine where everything which could be summed up as "survival" had been down to me alone.

I was all too familiar with men's need to exert their individuality in a group – most commonly manifested by the behavioural tactic of "showing off". With relatively little on their minds other than keeping the A.T.S.V. in sight, boredom would lead to frustration and careless riding. In my heart I knew that even if SMT caught on, one day I'd have to face the inevitability of a serious injury to one of the riders, unfettered by the self-serving paranoia which guided my solo trips. Anyway, the utter failure of the advertising campaign made the prospect of an annual SMT brochure unlikely and I was pleased to accept that this trip would be an interesting, experimental one-off.

With the day-before-departure crises which typify the start of a Big Trip hurriedly solved, the 101 set off from Canterbury one January morning, its camouflage paint scheme hidden under a mellow shade of beige called "Magnolia" which Woolworth's had on special. In the back every container brimmed with enough cheap diesel to get us to Marseille. Only once over the Channel did we find out that apart from wine, diesel was the sole commodity which was cost less in France than in Britain.

The 101 is what they call a Forward Control: like a Mercedes van it has the engine under the driver, or in our case, between the driver and the passenger. This intimate positioning produced a cacophonous din at normal road speeds that drowned out all but high pitched yelling between occupants who instead donned BSI-approved ear defenders rated at 110 decibels. In this state Clive and I drove across the frosted countryside of northern France, sleeping discretely in lay-bys or on wasteland to freewheel down the Massif into Provençe and Marseille. Here the gang where being delivered from Paris overnight courtesy of Motorail; say what you will, but Sahara Motorcycle Tours knew how to spoil its clients.

'HI, MARK, HOW WAS THE TRIP, WHERE'S THE REST!!?'

'Why are you shouting?' asked Mark.

'SPEAK UP MARK, I'M NOT SHOUTING, AM I SHOUTING CLIVE!!'

'I CAN'T HEAR YOU CHRIS, THE ENGINE, I THINK IT'S STILL RUNNING!!'

The 101 was crackling itself cool round the corner, but clearly the three-day journey had taken its toll on our hearing. I made an effort to lower my voice, but it felt like I was mouthing the words.

'Everything okay, where are THE OTHERS!!, Oops, sorry.'

'They've gone to the Police, Bernie got his passport nicked, his money an' everything.'

That wasn't the least of it. Bernie had turned up at Newhaven to meet the mainlanders overnighting there, ready to catch an early ferry to Dieppe, the nearest port for the hundred-mile run to Paris. At the crucial moment he'd realised he'd brought an old, expired passport. Not panicking, he called home to confirm the valid item was where he left it and arranged for a relative to catch the next plane to Gatwick. Bernie tore up the A23, snatched the document without putting his feet down, whizzed back to Newhaven, caught a later ferry, nailed it down the N14 (his first visit to France) dropped his bike off at the Motorail station and apparently stumbled abroad the Marseille sleeper just as the whistle blew. What a run! Well done Bernie, bet you won't forget it again!

Unfortunately, once they got to Marseille my crack quintet of desert bikers hadn't woken up until their carriage had been shunted to the back of the station's sidings. As the

the exact route out of the city, and soon came the announcement calling us to the lower decks to rejoin our vehicles.

'Right, everyone got their documents ready; passport, VRD, money to change?' I asked, while calculating the chances of being recognised as a commercial tour and subject to some permit or exorbitant fee.

'No! I left mine in my mum's knitting basket. D'you think I need them?' said Mike sarcastically. Perhaps I was treating them like fools, but then the memory of Bernie's double blow made me wonder, and anyway, I'd soon learn the measure of the group.

Up ahead, vehicles were starting up and slowly disembarking. Home-bound Peugeots, pressed against the deck under mountains of rooftop baggage, were revved furiously for fear of stalling, filling the hold with light blue fumes. When it came to noxious gases, however, the 101 had plenty of its own. Its diesel engine had a protracted starting procedure that was not unlike an early aeroplane. First you had to reach over the engine and open a hand-sized flap I'd cut into the engine cowling – a huge improvement over heaving off the fridge-sized cover which concealed the motor. Somewhere beneath this handy flap, just within reach, was a small button about the size of a pea, distinguishable by feel from the other protrudences down there.

After holding the ignition key in position "x" for between twelve and fifteen seconds (too long and I'd burn out the pre-heating plugs, too short and they wouldn't get hot enough), I then pressed the special knob with my right hand, engaged the starter with my left, and pumped the throttle with my foot. I only had a few seconds before the big-but-not-big-enough battery went limp. With a tormented churn of the starter first one, then three, five, three and eventually all six cylinders spluttered gloriously into life, filling me with glee and my rear view mirror with a nasty cloud of carcinogenic filth.

It was commonly known to all but myself that this particular Ford engine was a notoriously bad starter. Factory-designed afterthoughts like ether-injection and special explosive cartridges to aid cold starts were missing from my engine, but with a learned knack and a Ford-approved assemblage of votive offerings decorating the dash, once the motor started it kept going.

With the mother ship ticking over evenly, the four bikes followed it out onto the quay to join the long queue creeping towards the Customs shed. By now all too familiar with the protracted sequence of Algerian immigration formalities, I walked ahead with the bikers to help them correctly fill out the various forms while Clive crept along in the "van", as I liked to call the 101. Inside, all Algerian vehicles laden with French goodies were being taken apart pitilessly while our group, clearly bound for the desert (God only knew why) slipped through with a cursory peep behind the van's canvas. Once other permits, insurance and officially-changed money had been collected, we were ready to dive into the free-spinning roulette wheel that was Algiers' daily traffic, hopefully to be spat out southwards across the Atlas towards the Sahara.

Chapter Five

Algiers is a capital I've visited more than any other and yet one which I barely know – nor do I want to. The antithesis of all that attracts me to the desert, I associate arrival here with lip-gnawing nervousness, and departure with "get me out of here I've had enough" exhaustion.

Beyond the north African limits of the Roman Empire whose frontiers were set around Constantine and the Aures mountains to the west, *El Djezzar* grew to become the capital of the notorious Barbary Coast. The region's eponymous Berber pirates, state-sanctioned and funded by the aristocracy, reigned terror on the maritime Mediterranean traders, reaching their apogee during the seventeenth century. The European trading fleets bitterly endured this scourge until the intractable Dey of Algiers slapped the cheek of the French consul in 1830, giving the expansionist French the excuse they needed to invade.

Within a decade the hinterland had been conquered; it took the rest of the century to bring a notional control over the Sahara and its trade routes, and another sixty years before a bitter war returned independence to modern Algeria. It was in Algiers around this time that Albert Camus set his pessimistic and socially alienated musings *L'Étranger* ("The Stranger"), *La Peste* ("The Plague") and *Une Mort Heureuse* ("A Happy Death") which together say as much about the city as they do about the late-20th Century human condition.

Since that time the stubborn regime of the potentially prosperous country has failed to match the economic success of its Maghrebian* neighbours, and a post-independence population boom has brought with it a mass of frustrated youth, facing bleak employment prospects. You see them hanging around the streets of Algiers – denim-clad and moustachioed, they even have a name; *hittistes*, loosely translated from Arabic as "wall props". Displaying their restlessness, boredom and scorn like a clenched fist, to a transient newcomer the *hittistes* present an intimidating force that quickly propels the traveller out of the city. Everywhere in Algiers you experience the discomforting realisation of having stumbled into the dodgey end of town, a feeling which extends to much of the north of the country. Whether it's the legacy of French colonialism, which ended in 1962, or the taciturn nature of the Arab population, Algeria lacks even the opprobrious vitality of neighbouring Morocco. The writer John Marriner, while far from sympathetic with the refractory "left-ward" shifts of post-colonial governments, gave the north of the country a much fairer trial in his detailed and thoughtfully opinionated account, *Sailing to Timbuktoo* . He found the Algerian a "sullen morose sort of chap" when compared to the Tunisians and Moroccans he'd also met.

It is this utterly disenchanted mass which has responded to the reactionary cry of Islamic fundamentalism, a movement to which the democratically defeated socialist government refused to bow in 1991. The ensuing bloodshed, in which 50,000 have lost their lives in five years is tearing the country to bits. Schoolgirls are hacked to death

---

* The Maghreb is the Arabic name for Africa north of the Sahara.

for rejecting the institution of *purdah* while Christian foreigners, diplomats, dissident journalists or ex-pat oil engineers make more predictable targets. In the meantime the government-backed army repays the violence tenfold. For Westerners, Algeria has become the Iran or Iraq of the Eighties, with the capital (and occasionally mainland France) the focus of weekly and indiscriminate bombings, executions and reprisals. Even as I write these very words a French radio station tells of two huge bombs in the Bab El Oued district killing seventeen people and injuring a further two hundred and fifty.

But Algeria's descent into bloodshed was not even on the horizon as Sahara Motorcycle Tours moved off in the wrong direction, corrected itself, and began the climb up through the city's congested streets. The bikes kept close to the lumbering, belching van, unwilling to be lost in Algiers' indeterminate sprawl. With satisfaction we filled our tanks using our newly bought *dinars* and, as the coastal conurbation topped out, followed the country's sole stretch of motorway towards Blida at the foot of the Atlas Tellien.

Once out of the capital and securely on our way we relaxed and took in our surroundings. Olive groves offered a singularly familiar sight and vendors beckoned us with their produce from roadside stalls. Small towns of friable apartment blocks and half-finished industrial installations rose from the red earth. At one, a half-built flyover diverted traffic through a dry river bed and slowed by the queue, Clive spotted a *boulangerie* and hopped out to buy a handful of baguettes.

'That wasn't too hard' he exclaimed, climbing back into the cab, pleased at the success of his first Algerian transaction as the expedition's catering superintendent. In Francophone African countries, particularly those of the Maghreb, French is spoken with the distinct hardness of Occitan France. Consonants are enunciated with a pleasing crispness, giving a Hispanic twang which makes comprehension much easier for sub O-level linguists like Clive and myself.

With only a couple of hours of daylight left, our destination that night was a grubby river bank under a bridge in the Chifra Gorge, south of Blida. For a while the restless bikes bobbed in the wake of the slow van as it groped up the stiffening gradient. But soon Mike, unable to contain his frustration at weaving around in a cloud of soot, tore past the van in flagrant disregard of expedition protocol, soon followed by Mark and, after a while, Bob. Pete stayed with the van, distancing himself from such gel-threatening hotheadedness and the trailing death cloud as best he could, until he too came past the van to take a healthier position just ahead of us.

'That's the bridge I think' I told Clive who of course, didn't know any better but was prepared to accept my judgement. I pulled off the road to check – yes, this was the place, a little muddier than last time, but still a handy but concealed spot to camp. We rode down onto the bank before any passing vehicles spotted us and chose to investigate, or passed on the news of *les étrangers* for some reason camping by the river when there was a perfectly fine hotel just up the road.

Dusk came early in the narrow gorge as we clumsily went about the task of settling in or rather, spreading out for our first night out together. People searched around for the few flat dry spots and Pete, long past the age when dossing on the cold ground was fun, erected his little tent to the mild scorn of the others. As Mark and Mike scoured the banks for firewood and Clive considered how to impress us with his inaugural feast, a couple of young men unexpectedly wandered into the camp out of the darkness, startling us all.

'Bonsoir' they offered, looking around the camp's scattered paraphernalia which had sprung up across their usual path home.

'*Bonsoir*' we replied, stopping in our tasks, unsure if we were infringing some municipal by-law or desecrating something.

'*Vous restez ici ce soir?*'

'*Oui,*' someone said.

'*Il va faire froid*' one of them observed.

We acknowledged this without knowing what to add, vulnerable and unsure of ourselves on this, our first night in Africa together.

'*Il y a des loups par ici*' the other added, in an effort to provoke our diffidence.

'*Ah oui*' we smiled ingratiatingly – except Pete, the only accomplished French speaker among us, who alone knew what *loups* were.

Exasperated by our sulleness, the two of them wandered on up the gorge with a *bonsoir*, leaving us to get on with our chores.

'Hear that,' said Pete 'they said there are wolves around here, tear a grown man to bits in seconds.' He slung his sleeping bag into his tent with a smug swish.

Irritated that our cosy hideaway had been so quickly unearthed, I wondered what sort of wolves they meant exactly, and feared an unwanted visit in the dead of night.

'I think it might be a good idea if we all share a watch tonight, in case those guys, or someone else comes back.' Waiting for ridicule to be poured on my rather melodramatic suggestion, only Pete grumbled a bit about the interruption to his night's sleep.

'It'll only be an hour and a half each, and you can keep the fire going as long as the wood lasts. It'll be the only time we have to do it – in the desert we'll be safe,' I continued reassuringly, as I wondered whether the watch might even help establish a shared interest in the group's well-being.

Dawn revealed an intact camp with Mark cheerfully stoking the fire up to boil some water.

'No wolves then?' enquired a bleary Pete emerging from

his tent.

'I thought I heard some actually,' said Bob 'there was definitely something howling out there last night.'

'Yeah, it was me. Anyone seen my fags?'

'You don't want a ciggy, Mike, you want a nice cup of tea.' said Mark, settling the kettle into a hotter spot.

'Fuck off. Ah, there they are. Shit, they're all damp,' he responded grumpily, flicking at his lighter. 'That kettle boiling or what?'

Although not being a breakfast eater by nature, I was rather pleased with the arrangement and variety of early morning condiments I'd procured for the group. The sides of the 101 hinged down to make a handy counter along which I proudly spread kilo tubs of marg', honey, peanut butter and *two types* of jam. Three cereals responded readily with a snap crackle and pop to Long Life milk and yesterday's bread, a denser version of that found in France, was still malleable. Of course how long this mouth-watering array would last without refrigeration in the Sahara remained to be seen.

As we tucked in, Clive chatted with Mike and Mark, who were already bonding along nicely. Pete huddled round his mug and stared at the fire with Bob at his side, while I started putting lids on things, eager to get going.

'So whe're we headed for tonight, Skip?' chirped Mark.

'Ghardaia, hopefully, it's about five fifty kays. There's a really nice campsite there with *hot showers* – the last ones until we come back.'

'Roger-roge,' he replied in despatch-speak which most of us knew, 'Let's go.' The fire was smothered, the kit jumbled into the back of the van and as the bikers wrapped themselves up against the cool morning, we had our first bit of good luck, the 101 started!

Although I'd been driving on the right for days and the left-hand drive van aided this unfamiliar activity, the lack of passing traffic saw me accelerate up the hill on the wrong side of the road. No one pointed out this fact until a truck came belting round the bend up ahead to face the crawling van in its path. Swerving off onto the left the driver blasted me with his horns and probably more besides while Clive quipped 'Keep to the right, it's safer.'

Conceding that this was a good idea, I settled back, pleased to be on the move and spotted the mangled carcass of a wolf which had paid a higher price for equally poor road sense.

As we climbed the temperature needle rose with us, nudging into the red – and we weren't even anywhere near the desert yet. Luckily Hillbilly Motors had carried out my request to fit a powerful electric fan in addition to the flimsy diesel's item which missed the radiator by miles and had little effect. When engaged, the electric fan fairly sucked the vehicle along with the drone of a hoover, but with a not so welcome dive in the battery's charge, which gradually recovered. These are some of the many drawbacks of meddling with the fundamental design of cars: what I'd spent on the untried diesel conversion was probably more than I'd have paid in feeding the standard petrol engine with relatively expensive fuel. I made a note to change the engine oil for something thicker once we got into the heat of the desert.

The few towns on the way south to Ghardaia are all ingrained in my memory from the many times I'd ridden down this highway. Medea, where Pete and I had realised we'd forgotten to buy motor insurance at the port and ended up paying twice the price. Berrouaghia, the fog shrouded zenith of the mountain road: in '84 two guys had kindly transported my sick bike (like the 101, another home-made mongrel) to town to have its desiccated battery replenished. And there was the roadhouse where, on that same deranged trip, a French consular official from Algiers had burst through the door and asked whether I'd seen two boys hitchhiking on the way to Tamanrasset, the last town in southern Algeria before the desert crossing. With nothing to offer, he explained to me that two young teenagers heading across the desert to Niger hadn't been heard of for two weeks and the alarm had been raised. He asked how long I thought it would take to cover the 1200 miles to Tam.

'*Environ trois ou quatre jours,*' I guessed, not envying him the long run through the late-summer heat and sandstorms from which I'd felt lucky to escape.

'*D'accord, merci.*' he replied, swigging back his coffee and heading for the door.

'*Bon chance.*'

With that he was gone, and the guys behind the counter resumed their predictable enquiries and inane plans to emigrate to the great city of London where they had "many friends" and would I like to be one of them. I felt bad about eventually giving them a false address in England where we planned to extend our short but meaningful relationship. Was it any wonder I avoided social encounters up here in the north, I thought, although the help I was offered the next day in Berrouaghia proved that not everyone was out to exploit me. Now I just say I haven't got an address, which is largely the truth anyway.

The Frenchman's urgency had perplexed me. What could rushing down to Tamanrasset achieve? Weren't roving teenagers well known for disregarding their anxious parents' concerns, once embarked on their first big adventure away from home?**

After Berrouaghia the road levels out and crosses the *Hauts Plateaux* which sink inexorably into the desert and whose tawny colours recalled the autumnal Scottish Highlands. Ksar El Boukhari had grown enough to warrant a bypass and slowly we got into the rhythm of riding together as Ain Oussera was left behind and what trees there were thinned out and disappeared. Towards Djelfa vast seasonal lakes or *chotts*, only a few inches deep, spread out along the sides of the road like mirages. The result of run-off from the Atlas' southern slopes, they sink into the semi-desert's soil to feed subterranean basins or evaporate uselessly, leaving a thin crust of mineral salt rendering the ground uncultivable. Somewhere near these chotts I'd crashed while riding with Alain on that first night of my inaugural Saharan trip seven years earlier.

Laghouat was no longer the dusty old desert town recalled from that lamentable first trip. By the time our tour passed through its roadside checkpoints, it was clear the town had boomed as the government strove to encourage migration away from the overpopulated north in an effort to exploit the fringes of the desert. Plantations surrounded the town, but away in the folds of the Djebel Amour hills the Sahara's northernmost dunes could already be seen glowing menacingly.

Just south of town where the interminable plain of the Sahara begins to manifest itself, we pulled over for lunch. Unable to contain their delight at the vast expanse of gravel and sand around them, Mark and Mike dumped their helmets and tore off, flicking up stones with their spinning back wheels and sliding off harmlessly into the dirt. Pete, knowing what lay ahead, was disinterested in such showing-off and preferred to speed along the meal while Bob cautiously accustomed himself to the feel of his bike in the dirt. In doing so, a stone got caught up in his chain, dam-

** A year and a half later I received a sobering footnote to their disappearance. As the *douanier* in the dusty customs hut at Labbezanga on the Mali–Niger frontier scrutinised my passport, I stared at the already fading poster on the wall behind him. Beneath a couple of fuzzy snapshots of two young French boys was an appeal for information. The above named had last been seen in Tamanrasset in September 1984, about to take a lift to Agadez in Niger along the lonely 400-mile unsealed section of the trans-Sahara Highway. Nothing had been heard of them since.

I'd never heard of anyone disappearing in the desert before, and this sudden connection between the roadhouse eighteen months and as many hundred miles ago startled me. The thought of their bodies and unwanted possessions buried hastily in the vast desert I'd just scraped through was shocking. Since that time I've read that in one year seventy people disappeared without trace, having left Tamanrasset to cross the desert, although almost all of these would be ill-equipped parties, both local and European, who get lost or break down away from the piste and run out of water. As E.F. Gautier observed on this morbid subject: "The bodies of those who stray from the trails are never found, and they are reported only as having disappeared."

aging it irreparably, a problem which would have terminated a solo trip. Deciding we'd fit the spare chain that evening in Ghardaia, his defunct bike was speedily fixed onto the van's home-made bike carrier which towed the bike on its rear wheel. As Bob sat by the tailgate to keep an eye on this untried system, the guiding principle of Sahara Motorcycle Tours and its all-terrain support vehicle had already been validated on our first full day in Africa. With the fully equipped A.T.S.V and her highly trained operatives, an Experience of a Lifetime need not end prematurely due to a petty but insoluble breakdown.

What was also subsequently proved was the problem of driving in convoy. Further down the road I suggested someone visited a town close to the road to buy some fresh bread – we'd wait for them by the southern outskirts. A simple enough instruction, but one which was nevertheless misunderstood. The bread patrol had thought we'd tired of waiting and moved on and we thought they'd shot on without waiting for us. Whatever, the procedure prescribed in everyone's Pre-Departure Information was admirably followed and we re-united with the bread bearers a short while after sunset on the edge of Ghardaia and descended steeply into the valley-bound settlement.

The Mission

Ghardaia is the Last Big Town in northern Algeria and it can be said that from here onwards the desert rules. The telegraph poles which have traced the highway thus far disappear, replaced by 300-foot-high radio repeater stations every couple of hundred kilometres. It's the last place with reasonable connections with Europe and, for the desert traveller, a place to take stock, if necessary. From here southwards towns, or even just fuel and water stops, are up to 250 miles apart and traffic thins dramatically. For the approaching Saharan (my term for a Saharan aficionado), Ghardaia marks the end of "getting there" and the beginning of "being there".

The town, in fact five towns tucked out of sight along adjoining valleys, has an interesting history. In the eleventh century the puritanical Mozabite sect spilt from mainstream Islam and settled here in what then must have been the edge of the world and has since become known as the M'zab. The differences which drove them from their less dynamic Berber kin stemmed from the Mozabites' zealous propensity for the world of commerce, a Quaker-like interpretation of the maxim, God helps those who help themselves. Simultaneously hated and envied, rather as the Jews have

First Flatters
Mission - 1880

Ouargla

50 miles

Gassi Touil

Grand Erg Oriental

Gara Khanfoussa

to Ghat

been in Europe since medieval times, they settled in the middle of nowhere to establish their own version of the Mormon's Salt Lake City and where they could express their merchandising zeal in profitable peace. Ideally positioned to catch the best of the trans-Saharan bargains, they've been wheeling and dealing along the oases of the southern Maghreb for nine centuries and now are the leading *commerçants* in all major Algerian towns.

As if to underline this fact, *Camping M'zab* at the north edge of town was run with an enthusiasm that encouraged an extended stay. The walled and palm-shaded site, irrigated by carefully tended channels and sluices, gave the place a charming "secret garden" feel unlike any Algerian desert campsite. Like many trans-Saharans, we sorted out the jumble of gear that had developed in the back of the van, checked over our vehicles and got ready for the 800-mile run southeast to Illizi where the tarmac ended and the sensational off-road part of our trip would begin.

Pete probably knew those thousand-odd kilometres better than he wanted to. A year earlier he and I had been changing tyres outside Illizi in preparation for our first piste to Djanet, a remote oasis on the other side of the Tassili N'Ajjer. While tending to his back wheel he'd noticed a broken spoke, a heavy duty item which he'd had strengthened on my recommendation. Closer inspection revealed other broken spokes and several loose ones. He and I were about to cross the Fadnoun Plateau, a barren moonscape of bare volcanic rock which has been described by a well-travelled source as The Worst Road in the World, and it was clear that he could not continue with his wheels as they were. Furthermore, it was doubtful whether there were any replacement spokes to fit his Yamaha in the whole country, let alone Illizi.

Pete's first experience of the Sahara had ended like my own a few years earlier, cut short by a small but irreparable defect which obliterated months of planning and expectation. Forced to turn back, he was so desperate to get out of

Algeria before the Christmas shutdown that he'd covered most of the distance to Ghardaia in one fourteen-hour, butt-numbing day, arriving just as his back wheel began to disintegrate completely. With the stupefying swings of bad and good fortune which I myself have come to recognise as the essence of the Saharan experience, he'd managed to fly with his sickly bike as "excess baggage" to Algiers for just £40, and got to Dover for Christmas – not quite his native Liverpool but good enough.

As on my first aborted trip, he'd fled north with a great urgency, escaping from the menacing desert like a scene in a thriller when the hero bolts down a corridor of successively closing hatches, nipping through them just as they slam shut. Pete had tried to ride across the Sahara with me and failed through no fault of his own – he could file the whole escapade under "Stories to tell my grandchildren" and get on with something else. But like myself he'd also forgotten the miseries, learned a lot and harboured a nagging curiosity about what he'd missed. And as he was soon to discover, he'd had to turn back at the start of one of the country's most spectacular pistes leading to its most beautiful region, the Tassili N'Ajjer.

Brimming with the essential fluids of fuel and water and a few scrawny vegetables we'd bought in town, the 101 crawled out of the ravine in which the Mozabite towns huddle, letting the bikes speed off up the hill. In a few miles we turned east off the trans-Saharan Highway (as the Algiers–Tamanrasset road is known) and headed for the oil towns which mark Algeria's eastern flank. An untypical westerly wind helped us along under a gray sky which promised rain, but which dissipated in an hour under the warming sun – this being the Sahara after all. All around was a flat gravel plain with patches of sand along which Mike and Mark raced, sharpening their dirt-riding skills and occasionally getting out of shape as they hit an unexpected hole.

It looked fun, bombing along without all the junk I was used to carrying on my own solo trips, but to me it also felt somehow irrelevant. Without the van and all its resources they wouldn't be here, and if they were alone they'd certainly make the most of a good tarmac road while they could, or slowly get a feel for their cumbersome bikes in the dirt. Later in the trip I developed a mild envy of the bikers who I felt, rightly or wrongly, didn't know how lucky they were to be gunning around the Sahara in such a carefree manner. It was great fun I thought, but it wasn't the Real Thing where you're alone, dependant on your own resources and accountable for your own errors.

After a while Bob tentatively joined them, but found the 50mph off-road pace a bit much. He slowed right down and rejoined Pete who was happy on the road and who knew there'd be plenty of loose stuff later on. Although he'd criss-crossed Europe several times on big touring bikes, Pete was a tense off-road rider, lacking the younger two's panache.

When not driving or in the mood to sustain a high deci-bel conversation, Clive was in the habit of taking a nap by settling into his ear defenders and tying his head via a cushion to the overhead roll bar which was fixed to a plate behind his seat. Any full-on four-wheel drive has one of these; it signifies that, not only are you the adventuresome owner of an off-road vehicle, but that you frequently drive it to the LIMITS!, risking a cab-crushing tumble which demands the security of a roll bar. In fact experience has proved this feature to be useless when, in the mid-Seventies, a 101 on a trans-Saharan military expedition drove into a hut which gently folded back the poorly designed bar. Any overturning our 101 undertook would quickly flatten us into a couple of wriggly-limbed dash-board pizzas.

By lunchtime we had come off a plateau and descended into Ouargla, an uninspiring old town that was now just a point on the oil pipeline network, diminuated by the bigger settlements of Ghardaia and Hassi Messaoud to the east. In the middle of the nineteenth century Ouargla had been more prominent, the southernmost outpost of the French North African colony, beyond which you were on your own, at the mercy of bloodthirsty Tuareg, unknown wells and uncharted pistes leading south for 1500 miles to the Sudan.[*]

It was from Ouargla that several explorers and adventurers set out into the hostile desert, many to meet robbery and barbarous deaths at the hands of the desert tribes who traditionally saw strangers as a threat to their autonomy. And it was to Ouargla that a dozen demented survivors from the *Mission Flatters* returned in April of 1881, barely able to speak of the horrors they'd endured. The adventures of *Sahara Motorcycle Tours* may well be gripping, but the ruination of Colonel Paul Flatters and his men, along with the colonial aspiration they sought to fulfil, is a gruesome story well worth telling.

Europe in 1880 and the Scramble for Africa was in top gear with the main players destined to settle on the continental partition in five years time. The Dutch had the Cape and Germany was set to annex Southwest Africa in a couple of years. The British weren't far away, entrenched with the Zulu nation in the Natal, while General Gordon was busy civilising the Sudanese and the northern approaches to East Africa. Here and there, tiny enclaves of Portugal's imploded maritime empire dotted the shores of the continent from Zanzibar to Cabinda and Bolama near Guinea. In the north the powerful Ottoman Sultanate controlled the area around present-day Libya while the Belgians were letting their missionaries do the hard work in the jungles of the Congo.

---

[*] The Sudan referred to here corresponds to the French name for the populated sub-Saharan region – as the Arabic *Maghreb* does to the north – and not the African country.

And the French? They'd grabbed a vast, and as yet, vastly profitless desert territory stretching from Algeria to today's Senegal. Revolutionary and international conflicts had bankrupted the country and so far the sub-Saharan *Soudan* had hardly proved to be the jewel in the Third Republic's crown.

The age of heroic explorers was all but done and one by one Africa's pressing mysteries had been expunged: the Niger river's contrary flow, the all important location of Lake Chad, the source of the Nile, all were now resolutely fixed on the continental map. In 1828 René Caillié, an orphaned baker's son from Poitou, returned from a gruelling ordeal with news that Timbuktu, one of the greatest geographical quandaries, was a decidedly lacklustre village of mud brick dwellings. In the west, St Louis at the mouth of the Senegal River had been firmly established since the Sun King's reign, and a few years after Caillié's return France invaded Algiers and its hinterland. All the troubled Republic had to do was securely link up these two points and stabilise the region as the British had successfully done in India. On doing this the vast markets and exotic commodities of the Sudan would assuredly be theirs.

But unlike India these two key cities were separated by the pitiless Sahara, tentatively traversed by ancient trade routes which brought up what black African riches the treacherous Tuareg and other predatory nomadic tribes didn't take. Unfortunately, since the French occupation of Algiers in 1830, these lucrative caravans had swerved away from French-held territory, instead discharging their precious goods in the Turkish-controlled Fezzan (Libya) or the Sultanate of Morocco. There had to be a way of conquering the wilderness and fixing profitable trade links to and from the Sudan.

This era was also the Great Age of Railways. In India, the enterprising British had clearly demonstrated the economic benefits of the steam engine, while in 1869 the "golden spike" had been struck down in northern Utah, permanently linking New York with San Francisco and the Pacific.

Impoverished by the humiliating Prussian defeat of 1871, France, had been unable to keep up with the pace of this worldwide colonial expansion. In 1879 Charles de Freycinet, a shrewd and patriotic politician and the new Minister of Works, was looking for a scheme to set France back on her feet. Under his encouragement there was a rebirth of previously derided plans to construct a 3000-mile railway across the Sahara to the Sudan, permanently linking the Maghreb with *Afrique Occidental*. The rest of the civilised world had clearly demonstrated: build a railway and you tame the country. Towns would spring up along its side and people and merchandise would move swiftly, safely and economically along it.

Anticipated problems of building a railroad across the desert were dismissed with breathtaking audacity. Shifting dunes which the track had to traverse would be magically grassed-over and stabilised, the dearth of indentured labour would be filled by "France's idle youth", artesian wells needed only to be sunk alongside the route to provide for the engine's and passengers' need. And the rapacious Ahagger Tuareg with whom no one had yet survived an encounter and through whose territory the railway had to pass? They were laughed off by the Chief Engineer, Duponchel as "a hundred uncivilised tribesmen armed with old fashioned lances...What was that against the might of France?"

Weary of war and perhaps appreciating the true measure of the might of France, the progressive Freycinet insisted on a peaceful mission. "Above all, go in peace. Show these natives that France does not wish to fight them...Let not a shot be fired in anger." Soon committees and sub-committees were assigned to quarrel over the actual location of the two termini, while the crucial expedition to reconnoitre the route was put under the command of Colonel Paul Flatters.

Orphaned in his teens, Flatters was a career soldier

who'd drifted helplessly into the slow lane of military ambition and stayed there. Thirty years earlier Algeria had been the place where unprivileged if ambitious young soldiers could make a name for themselves. But the scholarly Flatters had merely ended up with the Arab Bureau, arbitrating over petty disputes in the grubby desert town of Laghouat.

Superficially impressive reports on the Saharan caravan trade and a couple of historical treatises on the Maghreb had brought Colonel Flatters to the attention of the Committee. With his twenty years in Africa and fluent Arabic, Flatters' vanity responded keenly to their overtures. But not everyone on the Committee was impressed by Flatters' credentials. Addicted to morphine to ease his sporadic sciatica, he was described by one authority as having "...a nervous temperament, bad health, was well passed [his prime for] this kind of enterprise and had no judgement."

Nevertheless Flatters was given the job, although he soon disagreed with the liberal elements on the Committee who were keen to promote well-intentioned pacifist gestures in the Sahara. Notable among them, though exceptional in his unique qualifications, was Henri Duveyrier, who in 1857 as a young man of eighteen had roamed around the Sahara and had extraordinarily managed to spend several years with the Kel Ajjer Tuareg clan of the Tassili N'Ajjer region. His treatise, *Les Touareg du Nord*, remained the definitive account of Tuareg life and customs until the beginning of this century. A believer in the essential goodness of these proud and charismatic nomads, Duveyrier promulgated a discrete and fast-moving sortie which would pass through the desert with minimal disruption while making friendly overtures to all encountered.

Flatters the soldier had no time for this wishy-washy approach: European explorers were still being murdered all over the desert by the savage nomads, thought to be in the pay of the Turks who wanted to keep the edge on cross-desert trade. But the purse strings were out of his hands, and in the Spring of 1880 his compromised expedition set out from Constantine for the frontier garrison of Ouargla were Chaamba cameleers and provisions would be acquired.

Even today the Arabic Chaamba nomads who occupy the oases between Ouargla and El Golea are regarded as among the finest guides in the Sahara, able to track "the very wind through the desert" and accustomed to the open country with few landmarks and wells. Long-time enemies of the Tuareg, they were crucial in helping the French subdue the Sahara towards the end of the nineteenth century. However the suspicious Flatters, thinking them difficult to control and liable to incite tension in the anticipated Tuareg encounters, scorned their offer to guide the expedition. Instead he hired around seventy of their number as camel handlers

The colonel may have known the Sahara and become a sagacious administrator, but he had little experience in leading men and, it seems, little aptitude for achieving this talent. The quiet years in Laghouat had robbed his brain of any decisiveness and initiative. Furthermore, the first expedition had been so impatient to get off, it ended up leaving Ouargla in March, walking straight into the Saharan summer.

Accompanying Flatters were a handful of low-grade French officers and a mixture of *tirailleurs* (tough and well disciplined north Algerian soldiers) as well as the Chaamba camel handlers who led a column of second-rate beasts fobbed off on the naive adventurers.

The ill-fated group left the outpost in a mood of pensive trepidation and suspicion, and the situation quickly deteriorated until, two weeks out of Ouargla, the exasperated French attempted to confront the petty theft which had dogged the expedition so far. The challenge escalated into an absurd stand-off in the dunes with the expedition on the verge of annihilating itself when Flatters relieved the commanding officer in order to placate the Chaamba. The opposing parties contained their resentments and continued south, but within a fortnight the ineffectual Flatters gave in to a Chaamba ultimatum to head east towards Ghat in the Fezzan, rather than south towards their enemies in the Hoggar. The Turkish-controlled Fezzan was clearly no place for a French trans-Saharan railroad, yet Flatters acquiesced to his cameleers' demands for no other reason than the disgrace of a retreat. It was the recurrence of this astonishing indecision which was to lead to the ultimate doom of Flatters and his men.

Arriving at Temassinin (later named Fort Flatters and today, Bordj Omar Driss), he headed into the dune-circled peak of Gara Khanfoussa where he encountered a large band of Ajjer Tuareg. Attempting to mollify them with effusive gifts, he merely succeeded in engendering resentment from the similarly avaricious Chaamba who demanded a share of the hand-out. Arguments ensued, and discipline slithered still further from the Colonel's feckless grip. In the words of Captain Bernard, one of his officers, Flatters was "… almost in despair, he does nothing and no one dares do anything. In any case it is too late now." The Tuareg toyed with the unravelling expedition, sometimes generously offering assistance, provisions and feigned support, at other times obstructing progress or demanding medical attention and more gifts.

Eventually they made their intentions clear, forbidding further movement towards Ghat until their *amenoukal* (chief) sent his permission. The disabused and incensed French doubted their explanation but shied away from a shoot-out in which their Chaamba could not be relied on. Instead they turned back to Ouargla. As they retreated, one of the officers shrewdly recommended a face-saving letter be despatched to the Ahaggar amenoukal, Ahitagel ben Biska, proposing a visit in the coming winter. With this done, in Flatters's words, "phase one" of the *Transsaharien* expedition returned to France.

Back in Paris, the Colonel bluffed his way over the shortcomings of the aborted expedition, instead convincing the Committee that real progress had been made. They had not encountered "the slightest opposition" and the esteemed amenoukal of the hitherto unapproachable Hoggar Tuareg was expecting his visit in the coming winter. This time, he insisted, in opposition to the olive branch-flapping Duveyrier camp, the military presence should be emphatic – doubtless to help curb his mutinous cameleers as much as for any strategic need. His baffling eagerness to continue with an enterprise which, he now well knew, was fraught with still unresolved difficulties (not least of which was his own inability to lead effectively) has been interpreted as helpless, vainglorious pride. This was his last chance to rescue his life from the jaws of mediocrity and be commemorated in French history as the man who enabled the opening up of the French African territories. As for the reply he'd received from Ahitagel, but kept from the Committee? It read:

> "We have received your letter; we have read it and understood it. You ask us to open the road to you. We will not open it."

Amadror ~ Flatt's End

Despite the unequivocal rebuke issued by the chief of the Ahaggar clan, a hundred–strong convoy supported by three times as many camels left Ouargla in early December, 1880. Ahead of them was unknown territory where the only certainty was that they were unwelcome. Five French officers from the first sortie had secured other assignments and were replaced by eleven French men, among them two officers, three engineers and a doctor. Forty-seven *tirailleurs* marched with thirty-one Chaamba cameleers. There were also seven Tuareg from the Iforhas region (halfway between Tamanrasset and Timbuktu) who'd volunteered to guide the expedition. Typically aloof, they scouted unseen, ahead of the group and made their own camps at night.

This time the mood was nothing less than one of unreserved foreboding, with the paranoid and intractable Flatters now helplessly consumed by the ominous endeavour he was undertaking. He became reclusive and preoccupied, wandering alone at night and exploding in rage when asked to make a simple decision. The mounting pressure had squeezed him into a psychological cul-de-sac which was suffocating his reason. He firmly blamed the first expedition's retreat on Chaamba belligerence, but the signs were clear: it was the Tuareg he should be worried about, not the Chaamba. At the wells of Ain el Hadjadj the expedition had encountered some Tuareg and been reminded of Ahitagel's emphatic wishes that he did not want the expedition in his territory. Slowly moving out of their own territory, the Chaamba urged a retreat and, though there had been plenty of opportunities to disrupt the convoy, Flatters dismissed their wariness as another plot.

Instead, Flatters announced a facile attempt to outwit the Tuareg: by declaring openly that the convoy would head for In Salah, he hoped to draw hostile Tuareg forces there while actually continuing directly south. Five weeks' march out of Ouargla they reached the Amguid Gorge where the men soothed themselves for several days in a rare *guelta*, or rock pool. Meanwhile one of the Chaamba guides, Bou Djemaa, was despatched to make contact with Ahitagel and gain his approval. A week and a half later he returned, accompanied by the amenoukal's brother-in-law, Chikkat, who would guide them safely across the desert.

All the misgivings evaporated as this astonishing breakthrough was taken at face value, and on the 26th of January the revitalised expedition left the sanctuary of Amguid for the Hoggar, 200 miles to the south across the plain of Amadror. In the meantime the haughty Iforhas Tuareg guides were dismissed while Bou Djemaa returned north to deposit a conspicuous number of gifts given by the Tuareg with whom he'd successfully negotiated.

Ahead of them the open desert plain was mysteriously criss-crossed with numerous camel tracks – suspicious evidence of Tuareg mobilisation which again made the wily Chaamba nervous. But the capricious Flatters blithely trusted in his noble Tuareg escort. Furthermore he did nothing when his compass confirmed that instead of heading for the flat ground to the southwest, the group was being led southeast across the Amadror towards the shattered rocks and sinuous oueds of the northern Hoggar.

From this point in early February 1881, the new Tuareg guides commenced their tactics of confusing and wearing down the expedition. Again and again they'd claim to be lost, and insisted the convoy make camp while they went ahead with the camels to search for the wells. In this way the vulnerable troupe obediently juddered onward into the broken country of the Hoggar foothills, completely at the mercy of their guides. Worse still, a quarter of the camels were already dead, and an unseasonably hot spell had increased the demand for water still further.

Things became even more baffling when a Targui turned up at the camp, sent by the amenoukal to demand a huge sum to lead the group south. The confused Flatters who thought this matter resolved ended up paying the envoy 1000 francs and the Targui departed, never to return. The next day thirty Tuareg appeared out of the rocks and began wandering around the camp with feigned bonhomie, demanding gifts with playful menace and unnerving the exhausted crew still further. Flatters bowed to their intimidation and during the distraction two camels were slyly abducted. A tirailleur trying to retrieve them was attacked and only made it back when the thieves were thwarted by gunfire.

The tormented caravan moved on into the bare hills, where by February 16th water for the camels had reached a critical stage. The guides explained that they'd missed a crucial well whereupon a furious and exasperated Flatters was once again forced to make camp in mid-morning.

The Tuareg were now ready to implement their *coup de grace*. They led him, his French men and the majority of the camels into a ravine where they claimed a well would alleviate their desperate needs. The group was not expected back before nightfall and was to be followed by the rest of the needy camels once they'd been unloaded. In the slender canyon the day's escalating heat was accentuated and after an hour or two the crooked path narrowed, forcing the group into single file. The Tuareg guides were far ahead now and Flatters called out to them to slow down. Eventually the French party descended into a small ravine where the well of Tadjenout lay by the foot of a tamarisk tree.

At this moment Bou-Djemaa, the Chaamba guide who'd been sent on the mission to Ahitagel, suddenly reappeared on the scene, shouting:

'Colonel! You are betrayed! What are you doing here? Go back to the camp!'

Flatters again dismissed this as another Chaamba trick and replied,

'You and your Chaamba have bothered me since last year. Leave me alone!'

'Colonel! You are betrayed!' Bou-Djemaa insisted and as he said this the valley shook to the sound of the Tuareg war cry. Ever optimistic, Flatters at first took this for a greeting, but soon realised what was really happening. As they ran for their mounts he and the other Frenchmen were hacked to death by the stampede of Tuareg swordsmen. Others like the tirailleur, Mandini, escaped the initial attack and tried to regroup the vital camels, the booty that the Tuareg were already rounding up and without which all travellers in the desert were doomed. Another attack saw the few retrieved camels flee back to the safety of the well, and the satisfied Tuareg allowed Mandini's unmounted group to escape.

Back at the main camp the surviving officer, Lieutenant de Dianous, didn't believe news of the ambush, but nevertheless ordered the baggage to be dragged into a defensive barricade and set off to investigate with twenty men. Depending on which version you believe, it's said that on arriving at the well de Dianous caught the post-victorious Tuareg – by now ten times his number – off guard. They panicked and ran for cover and, had the officer been made of better mettle, he'd have initiated an attack in which he might have retrieved some camels. Then again a partisan French version suggests that the courageous officer and his men spent the best part of the afternoon trying everything

he knew, attempting "...infiltrating tactics, turning movements, a sudden charge..." but "...everything failed."
Whatever actually happened de Dianous did nothing and
consigned the remainder of his troupe to oblivion. For
without camels to carry the vital burdens of water, ammu-
nition and food, they were as good as dead and the Tuareg
knew this. For them the battle was over once the camels, the
commodity by which they still measure their wealth, were
safely in their hands.

That night the lieutenant ordered the remaining fifty-six
men to abandon all but the most essential items and begin
the 800 mile march back to Ouargla – a trek they'd just completed with the aid of camels and guides at around ten
miles a day. With just a few camels left, for the first few
days the wells were frequent enough, although food soon
became scarce. In desperation one of the camels and all four
of the Chaamba's cherished hunting dogs were slaughtered
and eaten. But the Ahaggar Tuareg weren't finished with
them yet. They shadowed the survivors at a distance,
watching their strength ebb away as along with food, water
too became scarce. The daily pace slowed to a crawl as
hunger and thirst began to gnaw away at the party's forti-
tude and morale.

Eleven days and a little over 100 miles from Tadjenout
they came across a well and managed to chase away the
few Tuareg there. After three days' rest they moved on,
even buying camels and provisions from the Tuareg who
were following them. A dialogue ensued in which the
Tuareg, led by the guide Chikkat's son, Tissi, denied
responsibility for the massacre and swore "on the Koran" to
help the defenceless party. He offered food, water and
camels – in such great quantities that twenty men were
needed to help carry the provisions. De Dianous saw
through this divisive gambit but, powerless, provided a
handful of men, never expecting to see them again. As they
left, Tissi gave the remainder a sackful of dates to keep

them going until the men and supplies returned. The officer's prediction of their fate proved correct – none of the men were seen again.

A week later the starving party came upon another well, again occupied by Tuareg who this time refused to move on. The commanding lieutenant rejected the advice of Pobéguin, his deputy, to attack, and while they quarrelled over what to do, their benefactor Tissi reappeared, bearing still more dates. The ravenous men eagerly devoured handfuls of succulent fruit and within minutes found themselves raging in agony as the offering, poisoned with the deadly *efelehleh* plant, took effect. Excruciating pains racked their bodies; men became deranged with torment and ran around shooting into the air or tearing off their clothes. Others just ran off into the desert never to return. Those Chaamba who'd suspected there was more to the dates than met the eye helped subdue the remaining French who'd survived the deadly gift.

The Tuareg were now openly camped a short distance from the famished, semi-conscious survivors and when a small group of these men were sent over to collect some offered provisions, they were cold-bloodedly butchered. Again Pobéguin urged an attack on the camp before they all became too weak, and again de Dianous, who'd inherited Flatters' lack of resolve, refuted the idea. Instead they dragged themselves another 25 miles to the Amguid Gorge, from where they'd left with such high hopes less than two months ago. As expected, the Tuareg were waiting for them, denying access to the water. This time the desperate de Dianous ordered an attack.

The exhausted party didn't put up much of a fight. De Dianous was an early victim of the well-positioned Tuareg, by now armed with captured rifles. Again there's the heroic version: the pitched battle came to an impasse so the despicable Tuareg dragged prisoners captured at Tadjenout to a cliff top and decapitated them. De Dianous rose up in indignation and got shot while two French youngsters, still under the influence of the evil dates, "marched forward to their death". The end result was that the command of the remaining thirty four tirailleurs and Chaamba fell on the single surviving Frenchman, the ailing Pobéguin.

They crawled north, Pobéguin strapped to one of the remaining camels. Several tirailleurs took their chances and deserted with other camels, some even making it back to Ouargla, but the need for food became still more acute and the last camel was slain and eaten. These bleak circumstances now allowed the expedition's most chilling events to unfold. Having returned to Ain El Hadjadj, still over 500 miles from Ouargla, three tirailleurs murdered one of their own who'd been sent off on some spurious errand. They returned to the camp with his crudely butchered remains, claiming to have killed a wandering sheep. Most knew full well what they were eating and for three days the group rested in the valley of Hadjadj, junction of a desolate and rarely used track which today's guidebooks still refer to as the "Graveyard Piste".

On the 25th of March, a month which sees the steepest rise of temperatures across the Sahara, Pobéguin ordered his men to move on. Of the twenty-six left, nine were too weak or sick to walk and were abandoned where they lay. The rest continued, but within an hour shots rang out from the well. One of the tirailleurs, Belkakem ben-Zebla, was sent back to investigate, but returned with no explanation, just more human flesh which was devoured raw. A few days later ben-Zebla shot the dying Pobéguin, and he too was summarily eaten.

Within a couple of days a shepherd came upon the remaining group and led them to the rescue party which had been despatched by the Chaamba *khan* (chief) of Ouargla, alerted by the surviving deserters. On April 4th, four months after the ninety-seven man *mission* had departed, just eleven Chaamba and a sole tirailleur staggered back into Ouargla alive.

News of the massacre and its ghastly denouement soon reached France and the apoplectic press bayed to avenge the nation's humiliation with immediate and effective action on the cruel Tuareg. But uprisings in the Maghreb and other more pressing domestic matters saw vengeance postponed and finally forgotten. Even the Khan of Ouargla's offer to send out a *razzia* (raiding party) against the Tuareg was turned down. The catastrophic fate of the expedition which set out to reconnoitre the trans-Saharan railway was officially forgotten about.

But in the public's mind the memory of the massacre by the dark forces of barbarism grew into a legend. "It became [like] the death of Siegfried or Achilles," wrote the Saharan scholar E.F. Gautier. Like Custer's dramatic demise at Little Big Horn in 1875, or Gordon's defiant death at Khartoum four years after the Flatters massacre, these events settled into the memories of each country as a heroic blunder which their histories would never forget.

In 1885 a Sudanese railway was built by the French, the first in West Africa. It linked the hundred miles between the declining port of St Louis with Dakar, the incumbent capital of *Afrique Occidentale Française*, and it survives today, along with the *Océan-Niger* line which connected Bamako, landlocked Mali's capital, with the Atlantic in the 1923. In Algeria a railway finally crossed the highlands of the Atlas Telliene to terminate in Touggourt, a hundred miles north of Ouargla and in the early 1940s the Vichy government found the time to give the *Transaharienne* a final revival by extending the line from Bechar seventy miles southwards towards the Tanezrouft. Then the idea was abandoned for good.

The Dune Corridor

With only scant worries of a Tuareg ambush and need for cannibalism while Clive was around, we camped that night in a lovely spot, wrapped in the croissant arms of a dune south of the pipeline which links Ouargla with Hassi Messaoud. It was our first camp in the wild desert, secluded but not claustrophobic, and after the short run from Ghardaia everyone was in good spirits. Pete helped Clive prepare the food and we sat round the fire fed by the wood we'd collected from the river bank on the first night. From now on the slightest scraps of dead wood we passed would be stashed in the van for the evening fire. While the group unrolled their bedding, Clive and I quietly agreed that it was an ideal occasion to perform our own light-hearted ambush on the group.

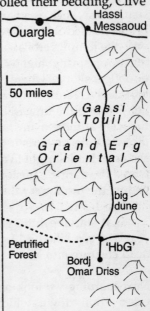

'Why don't you all go up to the top of that dune, we'll just tidy up and see you up there in a minute,' he suggested after dinner, and off they went, Mark and Mike racing each other up the powdery slip face while Pete and Bob saved their energy. The two of us pottered around the camp and as the light faded from the untended fire, we crept behind the van and changed into our ghostly outfits, Clive fetchingly dressed in a white one-piece number dug up in an army surplus store. Our plan was to crawl unnoticed around the dune, creep up behind the chatting quartet mellowed by the tranquil setting and fine food, and with unearthly cries that they'd remember for the rest of their lives, BUNDLE THEM ALL DOWN THE DUNE! It's what men resort to when faced with a quiet night in the desert.

Our plan went well and within twenty minutes we were directly behind them, ready to pounce. We took off our shoes and held our breaths, inching forward on our haunches. Closer…closer…closer. Then Mark turned round, saw us, and ruined everything.

'So, thought you'd scare us, eh?'

'Well, we nearly got you,' and, frustrated with our failure, we bundled them all down the dune anyway.

Back at the fire the darkness brought little gerbils out from their burrowed mounds to scurry around the camp. A common sight in sandy areas, these inquisitive desert rodents are incredibly jumpy, leaping into the air at any sharp noise, such as a hand clap. In German they're appropriately called *Schpringmause*. For a while we played games with the jumpy gerbils, seeing who could make the quivering mice spring highest. RSPCA observers would have doubtless shot us where we lay and after a while we let the harmless creatures flit around the camp. One of them hopped into the unwashed frying pan and began nibbling furtively at the remains, astounded by its nutritious find. I threw a mug towards it to shoo it away which, purely by accident, landed right in the pan with a clang that instantly scared the daring hamster to death. I was immediately vilified by the rest for my despicable cruelty.

'Murderer!'

'That starving little gerbil has been eating sand for a year and *you* killed it.' I got up and furtively dropped the dead creature into Mark's boot.

Next morning we took off for the fabulous run down the Gassi Touil down which the Flatters' expedition had marched around a century ago. The *gassi* is a natural corridor of flat sand passing a ceaseless line of 200' high dunes comprising the Grand Erg Occidental which flows unbroken to Tunisia, 200 miles to the east. At the inspiring sight of the gentle folds and curves of the infinite dunes, all of us, even Pete and I who'd been down this road before, felt we were finally approaching the desert of our expectations.

In the back of the van I'd stashed a bin bag full of what I called "morale boosters", mini chocolate bars and sweeties which were dished out at key stops, to help bridge the gap between meals. After one such booster break the van refused to start, emitting a horrible clattering from the engine. It certainly wasn't cold enough to flatten a battery – indeed the cab, or to be more precise "engine compartment with two seats and a steering wheel", was becoming hotter by the day. The spare battery which Hillbilly Motors had thrown in for free turned out to be incapable starting a game of Pontoon.

The bikes were well out of sight by now as Clive and I coolly considered the problem. Having owned a few recalcitrant cars himself, Clive thought the starter motor may have jammed. It was something I'd never heard of.

'Jammed? Jammed with what? Jam?'

The situation wasn't that serious and heavy-duty jump leads hung coiled in readiness to clip onto the next passing vehicle.

'Have you got a heavy wrench or something, I'll give the starter a whack,' he suggested, getting out of the cab and fluttering his T-shirt with a sigh of relief.

'Is that wise?' I enquired in a Sergeant Wilsonesque manner: "Mechanical sympathy" was my preferred philosophy while cruising the Sahara in my oversized Tonka.

'Yeah, it might free it – ah, this rock will do.'

He crawled under the van looking for some likely-looking component and finding it, thumped it a few times with the rock.

'There y'are, try it now.'

Amazingly the 101 responded to the beating and started up with its characteristic belch of black soot. Seeing as the rock had proved so effective, we decided to take it along.

We pulled off the road early that evening and rode towards the glowing dunes. It was clear what was on most people's minds: a righteous session of good old-fashioned dune bashing and a few hundred feet from the van a huge crescent-shaped slip face, the highest we could find, beckoned the slavering bikers. Now *this* is what desert biking is all about: cutting loose across the pristine slopes of a dune with no hidden obstacles except the steep slip faces which were as soft as a pramful of cuddly toys. Before I'd even got out of the van Mike, with the vigour of one who'd just found his pot of gold, had his throttle nailed open and was heading flat out towards the dune's right arm; Mark was soon behind. Once they hit the slope the soft sand devoured their speed as they dropped down through the gears, arching across the middle of the face *à la* Wall of Death and curving down onto the other arm to accelerate hard back onto the desert floor.

This looked like extreme fun, easy and only as dangerous as you made it. At worst you'd get bogged in the sand and fall off, or lose control coming off the dune too fast when the unusable road tyres caused a slight wobble on the soft sand. Or the engine, suddenly woken from its sedate highway slumber, might blow up. It was the sort of thing that I wouldn't have even considered doing on one of my solo trips. At best I might make a few passes over a low dune but this sort of brain-out riding, even with all the baggage removed, was far too risky to do alone.

We watched our two stunt riders refine their technique, taking longer and longer run-ups until they were hitting the dune, eyes streaming, at 70mph – as fast as the wheel-spinning 600cc bikes could manage – then curving gracefully across the face and hurtling back down. I took out the ciné camera: this would make pant-wetting footage for the

Sahara Motorcycle Tours commemorative video.

'This is fuckin' brilliant!' exclaimed Mike, skidding up to the van with a broad grin on his face. And he was right. Mark in the meantime had come off awkwardly in the middle of the slip face and was trying to get out from under the bike which had fallen down the slope onto his leg. Eventually he extracted himself without our help and rolled down the slope while Mike lent me his bike to have a go. Pete watched the antics, impressed but not wanting to try the big dune himself, and Bob pottered around, experimenting on the lower slopes of smaller dunes to see how his bike felt on real sand.

For me it was a strange feeling, riding with a reckless exuberance in the Sahara I knew so well and treated with such caution. Perhaps I'd been too cautious all these years, but then I recalled the many bike accidents I'd heard about or encountered myself. It's a well known observation of desert driving, one specially pertinent to motorbikes, that out on the sandy plain you find the going very easy. With increased confidence comes greater speed until the terrain throws up something you can't handle and you're going too fast to take evasive action.

That's what happened to Cape-bound Jonny and Adrian in '83, playing in the desert outside Cairo while waiting for Sudanese visas. Both bikes were fitted with the large aluminium luggage boxes favoured by continental bikers and it was one of these, along with his bike, that had landed on Jonny after he'd hit a small ridge and somersaulted. The ensuing night of resuscitation and vomiting of blood, the subsequent agonising ride in the back of an army truck, theft, and delays in getting to hospital had probably affected Adrian more than the semi-comatose Jonny who nevertheless had to scrawl a disclaimer, absolving the surgeon of responsibility should he die on the slab. He didn't, but his mangled spleen was removed and I've always erred towards soft luggage on my desert bikes since. Still, that wasn't going to stop me crouching over the bars and thrashing the living daylights out of Mike's bike as I ran into the dune at full speed.

No one noticed that Bob had also gone missing for a while until we saw him plodding back to the van, holding his right arm like a prize marrow.

'Er, I've had a bit of an accident, the bike's over there, I think it's alright but I can't ride it.'

While Mike, who had medical leanings, attended to his badly sprained wrist, Mark and I followed Bob's tracks up and down the lower dunes until they stopped at the edge of an eight foot drop. From here Bob had taken his brief flight, parting from his bike to fall with arms instinctively out-stretched. The bike had landed upside down and wasn't too badly damaged either; the clocks were crushed and the handlebars bent, but it was rideable. Unfortunately the combination of Bob's unusable arm and the beginning of the spine-jarring piste across the Fadnoun just 400 miles away meant that for him, the trip was over.

The animated mood brought on by the dune-bashing became subdued as we wondered what to do with the inca-pacitated Bob. Pete lent him his tent to aid a good night's rest while I fed him a couple of bootleg DF118 painkillers.

'How you feeling Bob?'

He didn't look too good the next morning. His face was pale with softly bloodshot eyes and he cowered over him-self like a hungover octogenarian, although it was hard to tell if these were the symptoms of shock or the potent DF118s.

'Oh awright,' he said, 'hand hurts a bit.'

His forearm was cocooned in a bright orange inflatable splint, an elongated water wing. It was part of a Full Body Set an English rider had foisted on me in Ghardaia last year, desperate to alleviate the strain on his collapsing luggage cases. An unusual item to be carrying in the Sahara, I thought at the time; you'd expect to find it in an RAF Mountain Rescue helicopter behind a glass-fronted case on which was stencilled "In Emergency Break Here". Breaking any major limb makes motorbiking impossible, or at least extremely painful, so the splints' practicality would have been of little use to their owner – it's a bit like carrying your own stretcher, just in case. Then again I'd carried some daft things on my first trip to the Sahara, like a months' rations packed into a bulging kit bag. "Ah ha! good thinking!," I thought, as there'd obviously be no food in the Sahara. Although, with the exception of dates, it certainly didn't grow on trees, I soon found that wherever there were towns, which existed even in the Sahara, there were people who ate, and that meant shops and markets and food.

"The more you take the safer you are," is a plausible but not necessarily valid maxim for travel in remote places. Equipping your vehicle with provisions for every contingency puts a strain on the thing that can hasten the very disaster you dread. In the desert overloaded vehicles frequently crumble, and a couple of German students I'd met carrying (literally) a ton of gear for their holiday-time dash to Cape Town ended up rolling their Land Cruiser in Tanzania. The excess baggage was given away or sold and the crushed roof sawn off. They carried on south into the wet season clenching a plastic sheet over their heads.

Bob wandered over to his bike to reassess the damage. Like all bikers, his principle concern was with his crashed machine. It's not uncommon for bikers to stagger, entrails in hand, across three lanes of motorway just to shut off the engine and re-right their wounded steed. Bob picked out a broken bit of speedometer with his good hand, examined it, and then tried unsuccessfully to replace it. He considered it again and then put in his pocket as Mike joined him.

'How's the arm, you can still wiggle and feel your fingers, yeah?' he asked with Hippocratic sympathy.

'Oh yes,' replied Bob, flexing his hand minutely.

'Good, that means it's not broken. Come on, get on your bike, let's go,' said Mike in an effort to see if Bob's humour glands were still functioning.

'Okay then, you hold the bars, I'll do the gears.'
Humour glands OK, check.

Three Green Bottles

Readjusting the bent bars on Bob's bike, I borrowed his helmet and we all set off back to the tarmac and Hassi bel Guebbour ("HbG"), a few miles down the road. HbG has a prominent position on the map where the road takes a turn to the east, but in reality it's just a hole-in-the-wall café with a few sand-reddened pet sheep and a timely petrol station. We stopped here for the breakfast we hadn't yet eaten: half a cup of sugar with milky coffee, warm bread and jam. Inside, an Elf poster marked the passing of a Paris–Dakar Rally and brightened the place up immeasurably. At this cool hour, however, the *terrace* was much more agreeable and no more expensive. The proprietor eyed up the flashy bikes in the doorway and someone spread some jam on Bob's bread.

To the west, a 250-mile *piste interdit* skirted under the southern edge of the Grand Erg Oriental, ending up near the ruined Fort Mirabel (now called Chebaba), south of El Golea. A year later Swiss Steve (who'll be introduced later) and I had tentatively driven along it, fearing capture and arrest by some errant army patrol, though we saw nothing for two days except some burnt-out desert racers. A day's drive from HbG the track passes through a "forest" of petrified trees, fossilised remnants of a temperate rain forest which are

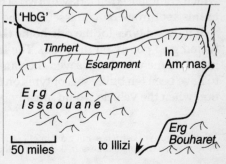

no longer upright of course, but scattered in fragments over a few square miles of the desert floor. Picking up one of the thousands of charcoal-grey stones, the grain of the wood can still be clearly seen.

Overcome by the antediluvian ambience of the locale, I dug up some unusual white fragments buried in the side of the nearby Erg. Close examination of the curved calcerous flake suggested a huge shell, bigger than anything I'd ever cracked over a frying pan. I assumed these to be fossilised dinosaur eggs, the post-natal detritus of the very creatures who'd long ago grazed in the rainforest, and which had lain undisturbed for millions of years until my propitious discovery. After a while I came to my senses; they were almost certainly post-Mesozoic bits of ostrich egg, common in northern Algeria until the hunting-mad French finished them off in the 1830s.* My specimen may have been unusually far south of the vanished Maghrebian flocks, but ostriches long pre-dated French colonisation when this region was less desiccated.

After breakfast SMT had some other digging to do. We weren't going to bury Bob and sell his bike, but instead stash the bikes' road tyres at a hot spring Pete and I had found the year before on the way to Bordj Omar Driss, now bypassed by the oil road. At the spring everyone was going to fit special off-road "knobbly" tyres which would make their bikes much easier to handle on the 1000 miles of piste which commenced in a day or two. The plan was to return to this spot from Tamanrasset, via the Amguid Gorge, and refit the road tyres for the ride home (knobblies wear quickly and grip poorly on the road). The logic behind this cunning scheme was that it saved the van carrying what ought to have been ten bulky sets of tyres on the long off-road section when the vehicle would already be loaded to the limit.

---

* Small groups of ostriches still exist in Niger's Air Mountains - and there are also complete dinosaur skeletons in the sands south of the Air.

Everybody enjoyed a wash in the warm pool, despite the faint whiff of sulphur and the strange punk-perms that the water gave to our hair. A thick clump of bright green reeds prospered in this rarely fertile spot and while we were there, some truckers passed through to catch up on their laundry. With tyres secretly buried and riders suitably refreshed, we set off east towards In Amenas, a huge reed flapping like an aerial from the rear of Mike's bike. A head wind had come up and a long section of broken tarmac, potholed and mashed to rubble by the heavy oil traffic, produced a ghostly dust through which we slowly weaved from bump to bump.

We drove along the edge of the Tinrhert escarpment, a two-hundred-foot cliff which faces south towards the distant waves of the Ergs Issaouane and Bouharet and the eviscerated mesas of the Tassili N'Ajjer beyond. Bob gazed out the window, drifting vacantly in his cosy morphine cloud. I'd decided to leave him at In Amenas, the only big town in these parts, where he could recover in some sort of comfort and ride back north when ready, a solution which he seemed agreeable to.

Next morning the pipeline we'd been tracking descended from the escarpment along the Col du Mouflon, and we rode into the oil base of In Amenas, or "Inner Menace" as Pete remembered it. A pre-fabricated single-sex company town owned and run by the Algerian oil exploration outfit *Sonatrach*, it had all the non-existent appeal of every other town we'd passed since Ghardaia. Lorries loaded with a single section of pipe large enough to ride the 101 through manoeuvred in and out of barbed wire compounds, and balloon-tyred *Sonatrach* Land Cruisers stood by outside vast hangars of machinery.

There was no hotel in town and so we unloaded Bob's gear at the petrol station and left him with a couple of stranded German bikers by a wall with a few rations, plenty of water and a spare stove. Mark knocked up a lean-to shade with a space blanket and a few rocks and, wishing him the best of luck, we departed. With hindsight, it seems a hardhearted decision; the picture of him, crouching by the wall cradling his arm and with a few tins of tuna scattered at his feet is still vivid. But the alternatives would have been unfair on the rest: to wait until Bob's arm recovered would take at least a week and to take him along now, either towing his bike or having Clive or myself ride it would have put an added strain on our resources just as we were about to cross the threshold from the safe tarmac to the uncertain piste.

As required for those bound for the deep south, we checked out with the Police; standard procedure for this part of the Sahara where details are radioed ahead. If you don't turn up they don't exactly come looking for you, but they might ask other drivers if they've seen vehicles matching your description. It's the most that the Algerian authorities can be expected to do; with the high levels of trans-Saharan tourist traffic (in those days, at least) a rescue service would be working round the clock. As it is, an unwritten code of Saharan driving expects other drivers to stop for anyone seemingly in difficulties.

With Bob abandoned by the roadside and the long off-road section ahead nearly upon us, our mood lost some of its frivolity. At the time it didn't seem that the bikes were being eliminated one by one by the desert *djenouns* (spirits), but the fact that the trip had lost 40% of its paying customers in less than a week did make the others wonder. Myself, I was just disappointed that my anticipated meltdown scenario was evolving almost to the letter. Riding the bikes on the piste would be a lot more fun, but it would take a lot more concentration too. Even without luggage and frequent stops, there'd certainly be little energy around in the evenings for pushing each other down dunes. And if nothing else, I was worried about the 101, for I knew that driving on the piste quickly exposed weaknesses which might go unnoticed in years of road driving. It was also a place where the labouring van would be left far behind by the bikes and I wondered how they'd feel about either crawling along so slowly they could hardly balance, or riding their bikes normally and waiting hours for me to catch up.

We headed out of town along the freshly laid tarmac which was inching resolutely southwards and came to another lovely overnight spot among the dunes of the Erg Bouharet south of In Amenas. While Clive rummaged around in the back for that night's feast, I set to draining the oil while it was still hot. At In Amenas I'd bought some syrup-like engine oil for the 101; it's what you'd usually put in an axle in temperate climates but in the heat of the Sahara all truck engines ran on it. Renewing the oil filter at the same time, I resorted to spiking it with a screwdriver to lever it free when it failed to budge.

I didn't feel comfortable about letting the oil seep into the sand, but where else could it go? There are no rubbish tips in the Sahara let alone recycling schemes. Everything is either burned or buried. (The eco-conscious Swiss Steve agonised over the same quandary when we were riding together, and ended up burying his waste oil in a spare inner tube.) With a bit of luck my oil might seep towards one of the many derricks prospecting in the area. I removed the replacement filter from the box and stared in horror at its threaded hole, clearly larger than the original, now mangled item.

'Bollocks,' I muttered.

'What's up?' asked Mike.

'It's the wrong filter, the hole's too big. And the old one's knackered.' The engine couldn't run without a filter.

'Let's have a look? Yep, it's the wrong one, the hole's too big, take it back. Have you still got your receipt?'

'No,' I said, for once impassive to Mike's tireless raillery.

'Well that's it then, we're stuck in the Sahara. Everybody, start digging your graves, the 101's dead!' he called to the others.

'What's up?' And so everybody came and cooed at the wheel arch where the black mess dribbled from the engine's unplugged aperture.

'It's the wrong one, Chris, the hole's too big.'

'Thanks Mark. Listen, I left a piece of sand in that dune over there, could you go and get it for me.'

'Sure Skip.' he grinned. 'Don't worry, we'll sort something out.'

'Mightn't they have one in In Amenas?' suggested Pete rationally. It was a chance, but unlikely. Ford diesels were unknown in Africa north of Jo'burg.

Clive, who had a talent for improvised mechanical solutions had a good idea; fabricating a sleeve of soft aluminium (plenty of that around, the 101 was made of it) which could slip into the oversized filter and enable it to screw onto the engine. Mike set himself the task of making the vital item, cutting and carefully hand-filing the ring with the patience and care of a silversmith. A side benefit of using malleable aluminium was that the engine's steel threads would carve a thread into the soft alloy, hopefully make a stronger seal.

'There you go, try that,' said Mike, blowing the swarf off his completed creation, underplaying the satisfaction of his deft contribution (but not too much). The tubular ring fitted neatly into the filter's threaded hole, matching it closely with the old filter. I gingerly turned it onto the engine, letting the threads form in the alloy, and screwed it tight.

'Well done Mike, you've saved our lives.'

'Think nothing of it, wanker.'

Next morning Mike, now resuming his role as expedition photographer, was up early, plodding up with his camera onto the spectacular rosy-orange dunes all around us, made especially photogenic by the rising sun. His tiny silhouette walking along a distant ridge made a striking image in itself, although I knew the reality of getting there was a lot of huffing and puffing. I'd been there and I'd assuredly done that.

There was no sign of overnight seepage from the improvised repair, but the pressure of the running engine would be the real test. It made heading for the Fadnoun doubly worrying, knowing that the filter might unobtrusively shake off, with a seized, oil-less engine being the first we'd know of it.

The five of us rode out over the soft sand away from the seductive dunes and headed down towards Illizi and the End of the Road. Clive drove while I hung out over the right wheel to check on the filter – so far so good. At times orange tongues of dunes licked right across the road like giant speed humps and at one point the road seemed to be laid on a cushion of dunes, giving the dreamy impression of riding through tangerine clouds. One thing was clear, the change to thick oil had done wonders for the engine temperature. Now Clive and I could relax in the cool and mildly muted "engine compartment" where the pressure and temperature needles remained comfortably in the green.

On the Piste

*I*I faut aller doucement sur la piste, c'est très dangereux,' the Illizi policeman warned as we handed over our papers inside the stiflingly hot station. *"Doucement"* was the watchword of everyone who drove on the pistes of the Sahara. Most accidents and many breakdowns were caused by speeding over the ever-changing terrain. The seemingly insignificant lack of tarmac changes the whole mood when travelling in the desert. Roads are predictable, functional and undemanding, handy for shopping or getting to work. But the unconsolidated piste signifies the end of civilisation's securities and the beginning of uncertainty and adventure. Whether on two or four wheels it demanded constant concentration and judgements; this track? that sandy patch? is it smoother over there? The irony is that you are utterly absorbed in locating the longest stretch of the most tarmac-like surface to avoid getting stuck or shaken to bits.

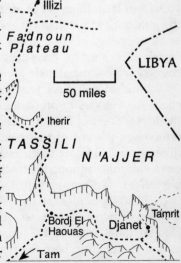

'Oui, j'ai déja fait la piste à Djanet ' I couldn't resist boasting.

'Ah, tu es déja venu ici. Tu aimes le desert?' He paused. It wasn't really a question, it was more a statement of resigned bafflement, why anyone should come back *here*. Most Algerians hated the boring, useless Sahara and the smelly, good for nothing Tuareg who lived there. Sure, for the policeman the money was a bit better, but he probably couldn't wait to get posted out of Illizi. He saw none of the desert's beauty or mystique, just clueless, swaggering tourists who got stupidly lost or drove too fast and broke their cars in half, or most foolishly of all, *came back*.

There were big plans to make the frontier town of Illizi a regional capital by extending the road to Djanet. In just one year the town had mushroomed into an untidy version of In Amenas, with all the resultant social tensions. On the wall behind the policeman hung a gruesome gallery of posters testifying to innumerable incidents: a dozen crude photos of long-missing or presumed murdered men, many of them nothing more than horribly shrunken cadavers, snapped where they'd been found, dumped splay-limbed in some edge-of-town oued.

We were given just two days to cover the 250 miles to Djanet, something I knew we'd be unable to manage, but the authorities were reluctant to have tourists lingering in the desert. Just move them on to the next *daira* (regional HQs) and let another set of officials deal with them. If only the authorities lightened up and practiced a little extortion as all the police in West Africa did, then they might not be so miserable, but for travellers at least, all dealings in this country were scrupulously above board.

By mid-morning we were parked up south of town to check the vehicles in preparation for the slow hot drive to the lovely oasis of Djanet, tucked into Algeria's southeastern corner. It's one of the most spectacular and scenically diverse pistes I know in the Sahara. Rising onto the blackened volcanic Fadnoun the track traverses bare rock, reducing those in leaf-sprung vehicles to little more than walking pace. Halfway across the barren plateau the piste dips into a valley or two and then descends impressively to Bordj El Haouas (lately renamed Zaouatallaz), the only settlement on the route. From here the piste comes to a dramatic climax at Djanet with the dunes of the Erg Admer on the right and the crenellated sandstone ramparts of the Tassili plateau on the left.

'There's the tyre tree, Pete.' I said pointing out the name we'd given the spot just out of Illizi where his trip had ended prematurely a year ago. The worn-out tyres we'd slung high into the tree's branches had long since been scavenged by long-armed passers-by. As he turned north that day to begin his race against Christmas, I headed south onto the unknown piste. Almost immediately I found myself seized with a mordant panic as the realisation hit that I was suddenly and totally alone – a feeling I'd experienced out here once before after parting with Helmut (you'll meet him later) with whom I'd been riding. I accepted it as an unavoidable psychological readjustment, a sort of "home sickness", and something that would eventually pass. After that, a contrary awareness of thrilling freedom and solitude would manifest itself along with that precious feeling of well being and infinite possibility – until some transient crisis cropped up to squash it all flat and you wished you'd never left home.

The details and landmarks for that solo ride to Djanet were taped to my tank – a straightforward run across the plateau without the route-finding ambiguities you get on the featureless plains. Nevertheless, I rode hesitantly and awkwardly, wobbling across the sandy oueds and hitting the rock ledges hard instead of yielding with the suspension.

After a while I stopped to calm down and let some air out of the stiff tyres when round the corner trundled two Germans on bikes identical to mine although phenomenally, if very tidily, overloaded. Coming from opposite directions, we eagerly exchanged details of the route ahead while swapping the customary "where've you been, where're you going" banter. They were nearing the end of a clockwise circum-Mediterranean trek, with only the rest of Algeria, Morocco and the Strait of Gibraltar ahead of them. In their heavily loaded state they'd laboured methodically for four days from Djanet, frequently having to push each other out of the sand. The brief encounter had helped soothe my nerves and reassured me: if these two elephantine bikes can make it then so can I, and with good wishes I followed their tracks and they followed mine.

This time with SMT I felt none of that apprehension, just mundane mechanical anxieties and a knowledge that everybody would eventually enjoy the ride on their unburdened bikes. As we got ready to move off, two soldiers from the road-building crew came up to have a look at us. Pete was in range.

'Ah, moto, Paris–Dakar, *très vite oui? Djanet ce soir!*' one said to him.

'*Non, non, en mange trop mal à l'hopital,*' said Pete, and he meant it; he very much wanted to remain "hang-ing on the wall". Not quite comprehending Pete's idiom the soldier continued, teasing the trepidation in Pete's caution.

'*Il y a beaucoup de sable plus loin.*'

'*Ah bon,*' said Pete phelgmatically.

'*Tu as du whisky, Jonnie Wokeur?*' the soldier provoked.

'*Non, il a beaucoup de whisky,*' Pete nodded towards Mark, who was keen to attack the piste.

'What, *moi*? No mate, *non* whisky,' Mark fumbled in Franglais, glaring towards Pete.

'*Alors, bonne route.*' Realising they weren't going to get anything from us, the soldiers sauntered off towards Illizi.

We drove past their comrades engaged in the onerous task of surveying and building a real road across the plateau to Djanet. Articulated supply trucks heading for Djanet had never been able to negotiate the Fadnoun's hairpins and canyons. Instead they left the tarmac at HbG and took a long sandy detour to the west via Amguid before cutting back east under the Tassili's southern edge; twice the distance of the Fadnoun route. Djanet's strategic position close to Libya, Chad and Niger also made a direct connection desirable, as did the tourist potential of the Tassili, of which more later.

The ascent on to the Fadnoun plateau began immediately with sharp-edged lips of rock slowing the 101 to walking pace while the agile bikes were already dusty specks on the horizon. We'd agreed to let them ride on for an hour and then wait for the van to catch up. If anything was going to break the van it would be this piste, so I nursed it gently along the brutal blackened moonscape, rarely getting beyond second gear.

Now that we were further south daytime temperatures were considerably warmer, an impression accentuated by our slow pace and the bleak, burnt-out landscape of hardened lava around us. It took the van three hours to catch up with the bikes, and then followed another three hour slog during which Mark changed places with Clive to enjoy a rest in the van. We finally reached the trio parked up on an area of flat broken rock, where Clive had used the time creatively to sculpt a remarkable full-size throne from the slabs of ochre rock. It would have made a surreal landmark on the plateau, more memorable than the car wrecks or distinctive outcrops usually referred to in the guidebooks, but there was no sign of it when I passed this way a year later.

We'd reached the plateau top where the track flattened off, enabling the van to nearly keep up with the bikes and as the sun dropped to the west we came to a rest in the shelter of a gorge, having covered less than fifty miles. Sunset came early in the valley and there was little wood for a fire or energy to find some. A shy Swiss couple in a Land Rover had also found this the best of a grim selection of campsites, but made it clear they wanted to keep to themselves. It's an odd situation which the gregarious Africans must find perplexing: two groups camped side by side in the desolation, but ignoring each other. In Africa the concept of privacy as we know it in the West is unknown. Why someone should want to be alone when there are plenty of people around would be quite mystifying.

Next morning, we had cause to be grateful that the Land Rover was there, as the combination of extra thick engine oil and a cool night on the plateau were just too much for the 101's battery. Wary of risking damaging their own battery, I assured the unwilling Swiss driver that as long as his engine was running, it would keep doing so while the leads were attached. The van's sludge-filled engine churned laboriously while he anxiously revved his engine. The pressurised ether injection or explosive cartridges would have been handy here, but eventually the engine fired on most and then all of its cylinders. Wishing us well the Swiss pair sped off before they became caught up in towing the poorly 101 out of the steep gorge.

While the engine rumbled itself warm, we refuelled the bikes, shoved all the gear in the back and followed the Swiss. Such reluctance to get involved in other peoples' problems is paradoxically evident on the piste, where assistance is all the more crucial. On the piste there's a constant sense of urgency that discourages lingering. As a lone tourist, no matter how much you love being in the desert, you're always preoccupied with reaching the next town (usually no longer than three or four days away) before something goes wrong. When you get there you're relieved. You make any repairs and buy provisions. You meet other travellers with interesting stories, but by that time the bustle is starting to get on your nerves and you can't wait to get back to the desert.

From here on the Fadnoun loses its morose colours as the lava cap thins out to expose the ochre shades of the Tassili's denuded sandstone, carved by wind and water into bizarre outcrops and deep ravines. Bikes and 101 drove together over the passes and along fabulous canyons on a smooth sandy track, trailing long plumes of dust just like in the macho car ads on TV. By midday we'd arrived at the top of the col near Gara Inhadja Kli where the Fadnoun takes one of its occasional drops to a lower plateau. Crossing the southern stretch of the plateau is like traversing a row of tipped over books; successive ascents of a shallow gradient followed by a sudden drop. From the well-worn summit viewpoint the zig-zagging track could be clearly made out on the tilted plain below, a piste which I remembered as being horribly corrugated.[*] I zipped down the hairpins on a bike and filmed the van's cautious descent and then attempted a backfacing pillion filming technique, but already the corrugations where frothing everyone's eyeballs into jelly.

After the fast run up to the col we now found ourselves utterly absorbed in finding the smoothest part of the track; any short cut that could relieve us of the spine-powdering jolting was investigated. Then at one point, as the van diverted across a sandy oued, an alarming series of pops burst from beneath the engine cover. Thinking that the engine had finally exploded, I pulled up on the far bank expecting the worst, but an inspection revealed no damage or vital fluids squirting into the sand. Everything seemed OK apart from an odd vibration and an increase in temperature which slowly warmed up the cab back up to pre-oil change levels.

With the worst of the corrugations thankfully behind us, we passed an Arabic road sign which I guessed led down a steep rocky track to the Tuareg village of Iherir. I recalled Bob's wish to visit the isolated settlement, trapped in a hidden valley which survived on a spring-fed *palmerie* and an irrigated garden. The Sahara Handbook certainly made it sound a lovely spot: "a tiny Tuareg village in a lost world of its own ...an unspoilt "Shangri-la""; but not with a gang of rubbernecks who had little interest in the place. I could easily picture the commotion we'd cause during our brief,

[*] This infuriating and vehicle-breaking washboard surface which tracks develop is apparently caused by the unyielding suspension of heavy trucks.

insincere visit, the begging fostered by guilt-appeasing hand-outs from previous visitors, and the resentment we might leave behind.

A year earlier while travelling with some Germans in the Hoggar mountains, a wrong turning had led us into a similarly isolated village unmarked on most maps. Already suspecting that the suddenly minor piste was leading us astray, we approached the outskirts of a tiny village where our noise produced a tidal wave of ecstatic kids clamouring for *cadeaux*. The Germans were ready with handouts of balloons which they dispensed magnanimously. Within a minute or two the inquisitive adults caught up, confirmed our navigational error, and with a few more balloons cast into the horde, we turned around and left. The tough track to Iherir probably kept a few out, but I felt it was improper to disturb its celebrated tranquillity just to satisfy my romantic curiosity.

An hour later the van's generator warning light came on. "What is it now," I thought, "just get us to Djanet and then you can break down all you like." I stopped and crawled under the engine to see what might be wrong. A shredded fan belt explained the red warning light, and the increased temperature and vibration were also accounted for: the engine's radiator fan had somehow been stripped of most of its dozen blades, rendering the near-useless thing now totally ineffectual. The spinning wheels must have caught a stone and bounced it around the engine like a bagatelle ball (hence the earlier "explosions"), stripping the fan and damaging the belt and radiator which, fortunately, wasn't leaking. "Nothing too serious," I told Clive who dug out the spare fan belt from the back. That extra electric fan which I'd been promised "drew thirty amps" (whatever that meant), would now be working full time. And how long before that shook itself to bits, I wondered.

We camped in the sandy gorge of Tin Taradjeli, at 1200m (4000') the highest point of the Fadnoun track just before it takes its final dip onto the sandy plain. From the top you look down a wide oued towards distant buttes, with the track winding down to the acacia-studded valley floor which leads on to the outpost of Bordj El Haouas and the flat run to Djanet. It is this change of character, from the austere rocky canyons of the plateau to the swell of pale yellow dunes which makes the run to Djanet so special.

The following morning the 101 again decided to flatten its battery while trying to get the engine running. With no other vehicles around there was little to do except wait or try again when things warmed up. Any help from the tiny bike batteries would have made little difference, but it's something we would probably have tried had not a couple of Swiss Toyotas come to our rescue.

'Having trouble?' asked a very English voice. Steve was an Anglo-Swiss diesel mechanic and before attempting to help start the 101 he had a good look around the motor, cleaning clogged up fuel filters which I never knew existed, checking obscure components and basically giving the van a service which Hillbilly Motors had overlooked.

'These York engines aren't the most reliable starters, you know. I would have gone for a Perkins or Isuzu myself,' said Steve as he tested this and tightened that.

'Yes I know, but they cost thousands.'

I watched Steve dabble with the engine closely, hoping I might learn something, while the others explored the gorge now bathed in a sandy mist carried by the strong wind coming up from the plain. Caroline, Steve's Swiss girl-friend, sat in some shade with a cloth over her face.

'You know your fan's broken?'

'Yes. Caught a stone going through a oued yesterday, but that Kenlowe electric fan seems pretty good.'

'Hmmm, it's big enough. You ought to have a sump guard to keep stones from damaging the engine,' he observed, like a doctor inspecting a patient's innards, ruined by a life of heavy drinking and smoking.

While he worked, I established that Steve too was a

Saharan and this was his third trip to the desert. He was
heading for Guinea, a little visited country whose mon-
soonal torrents are the source of the Niger River. It's a
country that had intrigued me for a long time, but visas
were difficult to get for tourists who weren't welcome then.

'Right, let's start it up.' The van instantly responded
with renewed vigour following Steve's attentions.

'Might see you in Tamanrasset,' he said.

Steve's serendipitous appearance exemplified many
desert encounters where fortune emerged from behind a
thick cloud of adversity. It becomes tempting to romanticise
this extraordinary tendency to a point when you begin to
blithely trust your superstitious belief that things will
always Work Out Alright In The End, but the grateful
appreciation of fortune's magical hand is something limited to survivors.

At the tiny café in Bordj El Haouas situated on the south
side of the Fadnoun, I bought a round of drinks to make up
for the long delay. Five litre-sized tins were thumped on
our table and punctured by the mute proprietor. The bill
came to five pounds, but I tried to dismiss the expense,
hoping the refreshment would cheer everyone up.

'YUK, WHAT'S *THIS*!?' expelled Clive, nearly choking
on the swig he'd taken to quench the thirst brought on by
just half an hour in the 101.

'Dunno, tastes like …' Mark examined the can, 'dunno,
ah "Fabrikay on Libby."'

'It's prune juice, isn't it?' Pete suggested. 'Isn't that a sort
of prune/plum type thing?' he said, pointing to the indeterminate brown object decorating the can. Taking his cue
Mike led a round of "keeps you regular" jokes as the
syrupy beverage was washed down.

Outside it was already mid-afternoon and I suggested
camping in the desert rather than pressing on to Djanet,
two or three hours away. The owner of the café watched the
bikes start up one by one and I thought this might be a like-

ly opportunity to get some cheap *dinars*. I walked over.

"*Jour. Avez vous du change?*' I asked innocently, ready to steer the conversation towards breaking a 200 dinar note, if necessary.

'*Oui. Pour combien?*' he said, hardly registering any interest – obviously a good sign.

I'd done this before and knew it was important to make crystal clear just how many francs I was wanting to change and how much more above the official rate he was prepared to offer. In this remote tourist trap I'd bargained on five or six times.

'*J'ai deux cents francs Français.*'

'*Seulement deux cents?*' he scoffed.

'*Peut être j'ai plus quand je reviens,*' I teased. The only official way out of Djanet was back via Bordj.

'*Trois cents,*' he said simply, a little over twice the rate.

'*Trois cents?*' Now it was my turn to scoff. "*Un camionneur m'a donné six cents,*" I lied about some generous trucker I'd dealt with.

'*Cinq.*'

'*Cinq cents dinar pour deux cents francs, oui?*' It wasn't a bad deal at four times the rate and I wanted to be sure the figures were right.

'*Um,*' he nodded '*entre.*'

Inside he reached under the counter and gave me the five grubbiest hundred-dinar notes he had and tucked my francs in his pocket. His manner brightened considerably.

'*Tu as du whisky, des vêtements?*'

'*Non, mais peut-être je reviens aprés Djanet, oui,*' I reiterated in my ten-year-old's French, trying to establish cordial relationships for future transactions.

'*D'accord. Le taux de change à Djanet n'est pas bon,*' he warned.

'*Ah bon.*' I nodded, grateful for the tip, but not believing it anymore than he expected me to.

We headed off towards Djanet, keeping off the corrugated

track which the lorries and two-wheel drive cars were forced to use. Pleased to be out on the plain between the erg and the cliffs after our last two camps in the gorges, we spotted some chunks of long dead trees, and decided to make camp. The wind had died down as it usually does towards evening and the van dragged a heavy trunk to the campsite – a hunk of wood that burned all night but could have served a Tuareg village for a week. As the sun set and took the day's warmth with it, the huge bonfire's heat drew everyone around it. We lay on the sand watching potatoes bake or poking at the embers. Later I shovelled some reddened coals under the van's engine in the faint hope of keeping it warm for the run to Djanet

Djanet

Rightly known as the "Pearl of the Tassili", the town of Djanet is by far the most appealing of southern Algeria's oases. It sits dramatically between the cliffs of the Tamrit plateau and the Oued Edjeriou, along whose banks a vast date palmerie rustles its thick green canopy. Above this plantation the old quarter of El Mihan sprawls across a rocky hill, the adobe dwellings tumbling down like some cubist township.

Located deep within the territory of the Kel Ajjer Tuareg (the clan who had been so accommodating to Duveyrier in the 1850s), Djanet's somewhat inconvenient position beneath the plateau and the Erg Admer has ensured its low profile. As a trading centre it has always been overshadowed by the better situated Kel Ajjer capital of Ghat, across the Tamrit and now in Libya. For independent overlanders too, Djanet represents a dead end. Ghat may be only 50 miles away as the crow flies but it's three times that distance by piste. The only other way out is down a desolate piste leading hundreds of miles south to Bilma in the eastern Ténéré. Neither of these routes have been open for years.

Isolated Djanet's *pièce de résistance* however is its proximity to the most spectacular concentration of prehistoric rock and cave paintings in the Sahara. Displayed here, in the caverns and gorges of the nearby Tassili plateau, are thousands of tableaux showing, in graphic detail, what life was once like in this part of Africa. Some of them date back to 10,000 BC and, viewed in sequence, the whole collection reads like a visual history not only of the land and its implacable descent into desertification, but also of mankind itself. Not for nothing has it been dubbed "The World's Greatest Open-Air Art Gallery". Today Djanet has become an expensive backwater with an international airport funnelling adventurous holidaymakers come to contemplate the plateau's prehistoric art sites.

Apart from a few cursory mentions in early explorers' reports, the Tassili paintings attracted little serious attention until 1931, when a French soldier camping in the Oued Djerat near Illizi discovered paintings and engravings lining the gorge walls. Three years later, an expedition explored the full length of the forty-kilometre canyon, recording over a thousand scenes of men hunting the kind of animals that are now only found on the savannahs of East Africa. Giraffes, elephants, leopards, antelope and hippopotami decorated sheltered cave walls or were engraved, sometimes with astounding clarity, on fallen slabs of rock.

Inspired by these findings, a French archaeologist called Henri Lhote took up the Tassili challenge and spent the next twenty-odd years combing the fissured plateaux and cypress-filled chasms between Djerat and Djanet (as well as the Hoggar and Aïr mountains). His discoveries have helped weave an astonishingly vivid picture of prehistoric life in this region of the world, and the thousands of art sites that he unearthed have since been analysed and classified into historical eras so that a clear picture of both artistic and social development has emerged.

Lhote's discoveries were by no means unique to this part of the Sahara; such prehistoric rock art survives the width of the desert from Mauritania to Egypt, but it is the sheer number of these pictures in the Tassili that is so extraordinary. In part this is due to the nature of the local sandstone, which has been weathered into protective caves and hollows and may also have absorbed the ancient pigments, so "fossilising" them for posterity.

These days this whole area falls within the boundaries of the Tassili National Park (a designation which now justifies a hefty "entry" fee for anyone travelling in the vicinity of Djanet), and the plateau-top sites are out of bounds to anyone unaccompanied by a local guide. For your money you won't get so much as a introductory leaflet, let alone a shady picnic area with interpretive displays. As the plateau is beyond the reach of motor vehicles, visitors are escorted up the 2000-foot pass by local tour operators while pack mules ascend by an easier route. The sites at Tamrit, Sefar and Jabbaren preserve the most breathtaking examples, the latter boasting no less than five thousand sites recorded by Lhote and a crew of art students during an extended stay in 1956.

The oldest Tassili drawings date back to the Saharan Palaeolithic era 10,000 years ago when humans were nomadic hunter-gatherers, yet to master and mould their environment. Now classified as Bubalus Period art (after the African gazelles that crop up so frequently), these crude scratchings are little more than outline drawings of wild game being chased by stick figures. Around this time the last Ice Age was on the wane and the Sahara as we know it began to form, signalling the end of human occupation in the region.*

The Roundhead Period followed (from around 8000–5000 BC), characterised by enigmatic figures with large faceless heads and horned masks which were painted looming over cave walls – though who or what these images signify is still not known. The most accomplished

---

* Though it might also be argued that the desert has endured for at least two million years, Ice Ages being climatic aberrations which briefly cooled the desert, so enabling human settlement.

prehistoric Saharan art however was created during the Cattle Period (5000–2500 BC) by which time mankind had learned how to domesticate animals and had developed the concept of pastoral herding and the cultivation and storage of crops – the so-called Neolithic Revolution. As a result, the people were much less helpless in the face of the changing seasons and nature's fluctuating resources: food was fairly plentiful and people began to build semi-permanent settlements. Typical Cattle Period drawings depict women sitting by a fire and children playing outside a hut while the men round up the herds and take them from pasture to pasture, or go hunting for sport with bows and trained dogs.

Away from the Tassili, fishing communities inhabited the shores of vast lakes which once lapped today's dune-filled basins; most notably the Aoukar in southeastern Mauritania and the former Lake Megachad which filled the Ténéré (today's shrivelling Lake Chad is all that remains). In this flourishing environment when every hour of the day need no longer be entirely devoted to the necessities of survival, more sophisticated and naturalistic paintings evolved. At Jabbaren, a six-foot painting of a goddess christened "Antinea" by Lhote evokes distinctly Egyptian motifs while several other scenes suggest a post-animist religious development. With this stability too came the inaugural wave of the population boom which now threatens to choke the planet.

But as mankind advanced so the burgeoning desert also tightened its grip. Overgrazing on the increasingly marginal grasslands may have exacerbated this civilisation's demise, but whatever the reason, within two thousand years the contented pastoralists had moved on. Trade routes were established across the semi-desert by Maghrebian civilisations around the time of Christ and sporadic evidence suggests that the Tassili was on the fabled horse-drawn chariot route of the Garamanteans. Based in the ancient city of Garama (today's Germa in southern Libya), they threaded a southwesterly path across the increasingly desiccated Sahara to the Niger River. But soon, like the wildlife population that preceded them, the Garamanteans were also defeated by the encroaching desert, finding that the intensifying aridity could no longer provide sufficient water for their horses.

By about 300BC the camel had begun to replace the increasingly ineffectual horse and elephant as beasts of burden. Brought in from the deserts of Central Asia, the camel was to have a profound impact on the modern Sahara, enabling caravans several miles long to traverse the desert, reaping black Africa's resources in the process. Depictions of camels in the Sahara hark back to the simple Bulabus period, for by then the population was again transient, sparing little time for detailed illustrations. Post cameline art of a sort continues all over the Sahara of course, with contemporary depictions as old as the last passing and suitably-equipped graffito.

All this held about as much interest to the Saharan motorcycle tourists as it had for me a few years earlier. Why pay through the nose to trudge from cave to cave looking at badly drawn paintings when you could take it easy in Djanet. Several times since last in Djanet I've been on the verge of paying the thousand-odd pounds to take a ten-day tour of the Tassili sites from Britain, when once I could have nipped onto the plateau for a welcome break from piste-bagging. In a way this describes my own desert evolution; having learned to travel in the place in short intense bursts, I was now ready to slow down and experience it more closely.

We pulled up at the gates of the only hotel in town, an overpriced campsite known as the *Hotel Zeribas* run by Hussein, a rapacious old Arab, and his retinue of lackeys. The lovely irrigated garden of the year before had been cleared to make room for more *zeribas* (palm frond huts) and a concrete block had been knocked up as Hussein's fortuitous monopoly paid off handsomely. Settling into a vacant corner, we breathed a sigh of relief and began unloading the gear into the bare but comfy twin-bedded huts. It had been an eventful and tiring ten days on the road and everyone was looking forward to a couple of days of R&R before hitting the next long off-road section to Tamanrasset.

The Hotel Zeribas was an exclusive resort for all-terrain tourists from the wealthier European nations. The shy Swiss couple from the Fadnoun piste were there, keeping their distance from the protracted mechanical problems of *les Anglais*. A new German Land Cruiser sported an assemblage of deserty gadgets, including no less than two spotlights above the rear door, and here too we encountered the Belgian Lada we'd seen at Algiers' docks with that mildly embarrassing logo emblazoned across its doors: an angular outline of West Africa with "Bruxelles–Alger–Tamanrasset" snazzily connected by a lighting bolt. Such a bolt had clearly struck the rear of the car whose bumper and rear lights had been compressed upwards. A couple of middle-aged French women, dressed to look half their age, sat outside their tent next to a nippy urban 4x4 and there were a few rangy bikers, mostly German and Swiss, who eyed up the new two-wheeled arrivals doubtless thinking "Pah! support vehicle, what pansies". Swiss Steve and Caroline had come and gone.

Later that evening a couple of Cruisers packed with French tourists swung into the compound. We stared as a chattering stream of women poured out of the cars. Sporting energetically patterned slacks, fluffy blousons and gleaming white trainers big as bread bins, the daring ones flirted with their cavalier Tuareg guides who pitched colossal holdalls from the roof rack, while others remained circumspect. Just landed from a Paris plane and heading for the plateau, some were already tentatively wrapping pristine white *cheches* (veils or turbans) around their faces, *à la mode desert*, fussing with the folds as they tangled in the day-glo tassels of their shades. They took one look at us and, intimidated, repelled or possibly even indifferent, turned up their noses, establishing a mutual contempt; they, frivolous wimps being led like wet puppies round a ballroom; us, independent fat-tyred adventurers taking the daily slaps of circumstance on our cheeks.

Next day, while others enjoyed a change of clothes and a wander round town, I got under the van to have a closer look at its damaged cooling works. The plastic engine fan retained only two and a half blades although the radiator appeared undamaged. Borrowing a bike I did the rounds of Djanet's mechanics and scrap dumps, but all I found was a heavy steel *ventilateur* that looked like it had once powered a torpedo boat. In the end Clive resorted to rebuilding the denuded fan with carefully aligned, flattened coke cans held in place with rivets and wire. The finished repair looked an impressive example of innovative bushcraft and hoping for the best I bolted it back on to give it a spin.

That night the five of us ate out in, as far as we could tell, the town's only restaurant. Barely distinguishable from any other building, the dim interior was lit by a few 15-watt bulbs and stuffed with rude benches and tables. With a bow and a *"s'il vous plaît, messieurs,"* we were sat around a large table and given the menu.

'What you having then, Mark?'

'Dunno, what's *potage*? Mash?'

'Yea – no, it's soup. I think I'll go for the cous cous maro-cane. It hasn't got anchovies in it? I hate anchovies. Oh, and I'll have a Orangina.'

Everyone felt a little awkward about crowding together so closely instead of lying around in the sand with a plate on their lap. The meals, when they arrived, were sadly Lilliputian and as far as we could tell, all identical. Jokes were defensively made at the chef's expense. It was nice to eat off a table and sit on a chair but, with the possible excep-tion of Pete who'd been waiting for this treat for days, we'd all have sooner been back in the desert.

The previous year I'd spent Christmas in Djanet, much of it in the company of two very wealthy young Germans, Marco and Paul, with whom I planned to drive to Tamanrasset in the next few days. Heading for Cape Town in an old Cruiser equipped for every possible contingency, these two were nevertheless discovering that even having lots of money didn't guarantee a trouble-free trip and so they were holed up in Djanet with roof rack and battery problems. One evening Philipe, a skinny middle-aged Frenchman who was in the habit of walking around the campsite in a saggy pair of Y-fronts, invited us over to the airport to inspect his old aeroplane. He was immensely proud of his historic plane, a twin-engined machine from the Golden Age of Aviation, and was keen to point out the enlarged fuel tank which former owner, Lady Vanderbildt or some such, had fitted for a one-hop flight to the States as the war turned on Germany. Paul and Marco owned a couple of classic sportsters back in Berlin and were full of admiration as Philipe started up the engines, but I was far more interested in the view down the runway. From this flat vantage point some twelve miles south of Djanet you could clearly see the unmistakable conical profile of Mount Tiska.

Mount Tiska is the first, last and only landmark in the featureless expanse which leads across the northern Ténéré to Chirfa and ultimately Bilma, nearly 600 miles away. A waterless expanse of cushion-soft, sand, it was this route that I had persuaded an only partly cognisant Pete to follow the previous year until his breakdown near Illizi had scuppered our attempt. At that time I knew only a little more than him about the realities of remote desert crossings and it is no more likely that we would have made it to Bilma than if we'd have tried to row to Tristan da Cunha in an upturned umbrella. In fact the comparison of ocean with desert is quite apt and the Sahara Handbook certainly didn't mince words:

> ...this piste is so lonely that if a lone vehicle should break down it could be months before other vehicles pass by and discover the broken down vehicle and some dehydrated corpses. Travelling in convoy is essential in the Ténéré.

To my characteristically optimistic reasoning two bikes made up a convoy and anyway there were over a thousand balises (marker posts) at 500m intervals all the way to Chirfa. Not anymore, as I found out soon after getting to Djanet. Even travelling in convoy did not guarantee survival and my proposed route was now firmly *interdit* with all the balises uprooted as far as the Niger frontier. Apparently a party of seven tourist vehicles had left Djanet a few years earlier and disappeared without trace.

Even though I knew this by then, Tiska's ogee-curved silhouette still captivated me. I might not yet be on my way to the promised land but I could see one of the gates that led there. One day when the time was right events would shuffle into order and I'd have my chance to explore this special corner of the Sahara. It might just turn out to be no more than better-than-average permutations on the prevalent sand 'n' rock theme but that didn't matter, the Ténéré was an inspiring and faintly attainable goal which one day would be my pleasure to fulfil.

Back to SMT. Next morning as we started loading up the van for the run via Bordj El Haouas to Tamanrasset, a small middle-aged French woman hopped out of her Toyota and walked up to me. Was I going west to Tam?

'*Oui*,' I nodded, tugging down securely on a strap retaining a costly jerrican of diesel.

'I have a guide to take me along the southern piste to Tamanrasset and I wonder if you want to join me to share the cost?'

The *southern* piste? The *southern piste*? I'd never heard of any southern piste. Unfolding her 953, she showed me the projected route, a little longer than our planned trajectory

along the usual piste, but to me something temptingly new.
I was intrigued. A quick calculation revealed that the 101
could make it but the fuel it carried for the bikes might not
be enough. Furthermore, I was concerned about the untried
fan and the risk of overheating here on the hot desert floor.
She dismissed my worries saying that she'd already roped
the shy Swiss and two French women into coming along, so
our four-car three-bike crew would offer enough security in
the event of trouble. How they'd revive an engine welded
into one homogeneous lump was really what I meant to
query, but the guide she'd found was very good, he'd lead
us to rock art sites and fabulous formations which we'd
never ordinarily see.

Her proposal added up to a rare chance to ply an
unknown route away from the main piste in the hands of an
experienced guide. To the rest of my group it made little
difference which way we went but they were all prepared
to chip in a little extra to pay for the guide. It was settled
and we agreed to meet at one o'clock outside the unofficial
hotel on the south edge of town where Anna was staying at
a fraction of the Zeriba's cost. Oh, and could my overca-
pable Tonka carry a couple of jerricans; her car was already
flat on its springs?

Having completed our checking-out duties we pulled
up outside the hotel, ostensibly a low-key café but offering
cheap lodgings to initiates like French Anna and her young
son who had the unusual name of Dalek. I nodded at the
Swiss pair as Anna collected the money and passed it on to
Chadli our guide; straying off the relatively well-worn
routes cost money.

The seven vehicles with Anna's Toyota up front started
their engines and headed out to the desert one by one, excited by the thrill of the unknown and the security of being
with someone who did know. I revved up the heavily laden
van and moved out to join the end of the convoy when from
the engine came a horrible screech of splattering compo-

nents that made me wince with pain and groan with gory expectation. Fortunately the clamour turned out to be nothing more than Clive's improvised fan repair destroying itself as the warming engine sucked the tin can blades into the radiator. Again I insisted to Anna that really the 101 was not in shape to be taking on brave new pistes, but whether out of companionship, thrift, or my desirable load-carrying capacity, she insisted that the van would be alright. Unsure of her judgement but acknowledging the safety of our numbers, I engaged the potent electric fan with crossed fingers and tailed the convoy out of town.

Anna's Southern Tour

T he mysteries of the southern piste are not easily won. First of all, contestants must cross the sands of the Erg Admer, a barrage of dunes which blocks the way to the piste's magical wonders and where the renown all-terrain capability of the 101 would be assuredly demonstrated. An old tyre is the arcane marker point where one leaves the main piste to follow barely visible tracks over the firm sand of the plain to the paler straw-coloured powder of the erg's fringes. But before we even got that far, the two French women's little Mitsuzuki had inexplicably boiled itself dry and, despite close scrutiny of the complex looking engine, neither Clive nor I could locate the problem – its drivers certainly recognised little more than the radiator cap. Deciding it would be unwise to tackle an unknown route with such a temperamental cooling system, they turned back to Djanet.

Lacking such prudence ourselves, Clive and I raced on to catch up with the other two cars. But trouble wasn't far away for us either and, as the van neared the dune's unconsolidated border, it became resolutely mired on a gradient that even a spirit level would hardly register. Obviously the time was nigh for Low Range. Most 4x4s has this rarely-used facility, an auxiliary set of very low gears which enable a vehi-cle to effort-lessly ascend steep inclines and traverse the gnarliest terrain. Usually Low

Range is operated by a lever in the cab, but my van being what it was, I had to jump out and grope around under the gearbox, singeing my hand on the exhaust pipe in the process, before eventually nudging the relevant lever into position. Low Range gave the odd sensation of alarmingly high revs allied with negligible but steadfast forward motion and soon the 101 was heading on towards the others. Everyone else had been lucky, making the tricky run to the main dune's crest in one go. It always seems to work like that in the dunes: either you get up these sandy ascents in one smooth manoeuvre or you're condemned to an exhausting series of frustrating shunts.

As was the case with the van. Again it sank into the sand so again we cleared the wheels and this time I tentatively reduced the pressures in the special sand tyres to improve traction. The gradient steepened, the temperature needle crept menacingly towards terminal meltdown, the sand deepened and again the van sank to its knees. All was not lost. Shovels and hefty sand ladders were deployed and we dug away the power-sapping sand wheels and laid down the ladders, surrogate bits of firm "road" which the wheels could grip, propelling the van forward with regained momentum. As I was later to write in *Desert Biking*:

> "Getting bogged down in sand is usually the result of limited experience or of not reading the terrain correctly; of having too high tyre pressures or of revving your engine and spinning your wheel when you should have got off and pushed... Maintain momentum at all costs, even if it means slithering around and riding in the totally wrong direction."

At least I followed up with some encouragement:

> "As you become more experienced on the piste these events should occur less and less, if at all."

Very comforting. Clive and I got down on our knees and

dug away fervently to clear the wheels as Mike rolled up to help, saying:

'Madame asks if we have remembered to engage four-wheel drive?'

'Tell Madame that this thing has *permanent* four-wheel drive, for all the good it's doing us,' I gasped, secretly cursing Anna's forty litres of fuel we were dragging up the dune in short hops. At around 25°C, the midday temperature seemed relatively cool compared to the crackling furnace one usually associates with summertime in the Sahara, but winter air is throat-scratchingly dry nonetheless and our feverish shovelling brought on a prodigious thirst.

I let some more air out of the tyres, treading an unknown tightrope between the pressing need for mobility in soft sand and the potential risk of damaging the under-inflated tyres over rocks later on. I'd been reading too many driving in the desert manuals for my own good. A day or two later I flattened the tyres, moved the heavy weight right to the back and the 101 attained its celebrated all-terrain agility.

'Right, let's try again. If I get going I won't stop. You'll have to walk up with the sand ladders,' I said, initiating Clive in the quandary that the use of sand ladders presents: once you're moving you can't stop to collect them until you're back on solid ground – in our case the top of the dune half a mile away. I eased the thing forward, choosing just the wrong moment to recall a Land Rover mechanic's opinion on my chosen engine conversion:

"A 3.6 York diesel?" Pensive sucking through teeth. "'You'll blow the central diff'* with that sort of torque. Either that or the clutch will fry."

Mounting the ladders promisingly, I grabbed another gear and found the van finally floating over the sand and myself bouncing up and down in the seat, urging the thing

---

* Short for "differential", a somewhat mystical (but vital) transmission component whose operation no mechanic can explain but which frequently "blows" on hard working or over-powered 4WDs.

up to the dune top. The van climbed steadily until finally, with the engine's temperature needle fluttering over the abyss, I gratefully brought it to rest by the waiting cars. The others didn't disguise their boredom, kicking at the sand or staring out of windows, chins on elbows, until Clive staggered up to the van with the heavy ladders, his tongue dragging on the ground.

'Your turn next time,' he croaked weakly as he reached for his water bottle.

'*D'accord*, we are ready to go, yes?' said Anna, already starting her engine.

With some difficulty we'd crossed the threshold and so, slinging the ladders, shovels and Clive in the back, I followed the group down the dune's lee side. Before us spread the flat and commendably firm Plaine D'Admer, crisscrossed by the shallow paths of ephemeral streams backed by a distant line of craggy mauve hills.

As we cruised along the plain, slowly recovering from our hand-blistering ordeal, the convoy came upon a large crowd of people sitting around a stricken Land Rover. This one, taking a group from Burkina Faso over to Libya to look for work, appeared to have been trampled by a camel stampede and then robbed of several vital components. It had been here for a day waiting for something to happen. Thousands of semi-illegal migrant workers sought work in the enterprising Jamahirya until Ghaddafi, in a fit of pique following an assassination attempt in 1995, expelled all the Palestinians, half a million Sudanese and as many West Africans, blaming the latter group for rising unemployment. Unfortunately the sanctions still imposed on Libya at that time made it impossible to ship this unwanted mass out of the country and so they've remained stranded in refugee camps for months while the paranoid Colonel withdraws into increasing isolation.

The Burkinese car was the sort of thing that gives Land Rover its legendary good name. Although certain models are designated as "twelve seaters" it's merely a well known "minibus" road tax dodge; no one in their right mind would expect to carry more than nine passengers and their baggage in such a vehicle. This lopsided jalopy was attempting to transport *thirteen* people and all their belongings, having in the process run it's engine out of oil and water. Although these migrants were now marooned only a couple of hours drive from Djanet, this piste was so rarely travelled that they might just as well have been on the moon. With typical fatalism, no one seemed very bothered, let alone delighted to see us.

We milled around the Rover marvelling at how this dilapidated wreck had made it so close to its destination; had it been a tourist vehicle stuck here our admiration would have swung closer to scorn at their utter stupidity and carelessness. The driver explained his needs and we topped up the radiator – sealed with a plastic bag and a rubber band – and gave them a spare container of water plus some oil which the car was also devouring – the desert in their wake was littered with their discarded oil cans. With their fluids replenished we stood clear as some of the passengers pushed the car back to life and bundled into the back to grab the best of the available room. Lacking a front prop shaft so giving it permanent *two*-wheel drive, they'd soon be back in the sand shoving the wreck up and over the erg ahead, but if they made it to Djanet, Libya was only a day away.

The irritating thing about joining a guided convoy is that you feel somehow removed from your surroundings. Divested of all navigational responsibilities, you become concerned only with the simple task of keeping up with the vehicles ahead. For the whole four days with Chadli, who took countless turns and detours on a myriad of interconnecting tracks, I had the odd feeling of being permanently lost and yet out of danger. Unprepared for this unexpected diversion, I hadn't had a chance to study any maps and only recalled him mentioning the wells of Tiririne, possibly Tadant and Tin-Tarabine; enough 'T's to make anyone incontinent. I missed the complete though often taxing involvement of travelling independently or even just talking with the guide and learning about the area.

The flat run across the plain ended at a small outcrop where we camped. A full moon rose early in the evening as the three groups made their own eating arrangements; Anna and Dalek with the guide, and the Swiss a fitting distance away. After we ate I went over to talk with Anna and chat up the guide.

Chadli was not a Targui as I'd originally thought, but a Chaamba, the Arab tribe from the Ouargla area who are much respected for their guiding skills (and had been involved in the disastrous Flatters missions). Chadli was way out of his tribal territory here in the Tassili-Hoggar, but these days such transgression no longer resulted in a grizzly death and a vengeful *razzia*. Chadli didn't wear the Tuareg *litham* (veil) but a simple blue *cheche* wrapped into a turban, an old anorak and baggy trousers with no shoes.

Guides, proper guides that is, not young pretenders, maintain a sedulous and aloof demeanour which, it seems from reading accounts of past travels, hasn't changed for centuries. They take great pains to assert their separateness from their clients, and they appear to eat virtually nothing, turning down offers of food to the point where you start thinking either that they might faint at any minute or else that they must have a secret stash of high protein rations. Never, ever will guides be seen doing anything as crass as drinking wholeheartedly from a water bottle. At best they'll be satisfied to sip some tiny glasses of tea at each end of the day. A guide's taciturn formality is only won over very slowly, revealing in droplets their vast knowledge and as little as possible of their personal circumstances.

It is this incommunicativeness which can often make those being guided feel that either they are being tricked into following an unnecessarily difficult route or that they have inadvertently strayed from the piste. Both on this trip and another time in Mauritania I encountered this suspicion and hostility at the guide's hesitation after backtracking to correct a momentary mistake along a 350-mile stretch of piste. This brief exhibition of fallibility might even be a ruse to rattle the convoy into realising that the guide's judgement should not be taken for granted and sometimes even he has to work out the right way, *that's* how tough it is.

Guides rarely have much luggage, usually just a tiny bundle containing twenty or thirty peanuts, a tiny kettle for making tea, and some deliveries. While we punters unfold our camp beds and pant into our air bed, guides will sleep alone in some ditch with the humblest of bedding; Chadli simply lay on the ground wrapped in a plastic sheet. In such small ways do the guides gently rub their nomadic austerity in your comfort-addled face. Guides regard a map with the same disdain or even puzzlement they preserve for all crafty western "gadgets". They actually know the piste intimately and depend on their uncanny memories and a number of natural clues such as prevailing winds, the colour and texture of sand and a particular type of rock or plant. They are as utterly in their element as you are lost without them.

Recognising that a dependable guide would be a valuable contact for later trips, I asked Chadli about other routes between the Tam–Djanet line and the Niger border.

'There are many routes,' he waved his hand impatiently *'vers Tirinine, vers In Ebeggi, vers In Azaoua. Il y a beaucoup.'*

He was typically unforthcoming. It was a diffidence I recognised in nomadic peoples but I was eager to show that, like Anna, I was an enthusiast for the desert, eager to explore its mysteries and get close to its nature. By swapping camps in the evenings, I attempted to distance myself from my lot who, quite reasonably, lacked my commitment to the place.

But it was Anna, who lived in Algiers with her half-

Algerian son, and not Chadli who took pity on my enthusiasm and explained how she hoped to visit several prehistoric art sites, armed as she was with a fully illustrated copy of one of Lhote's books. By the end of the trip I got to like Anna. In my experience it's common for men to see the desert as a place of challenges; tricky techniques to be mastered, natty vehicle mods to be validated or tough pistes to be unravelled. Women on the other hand, particularly those doing their own trips rather than participating as co-driver or cook in someone else's, have a less confrontational and far less techno-mechanical attitude to Saharan travel. For them, or at least for the ones I've encountered, the angle is "being there" and not "getting there and beating it".

Next day we continued across the flat plain, actually the former flood plain of the infrequent Oued Tafassasset which once drained into the prehistoric Lake Megachad. Every principal desert mountain range has an accompanying dune basin nearby: here it was the Hoggar, which once filled the Ténéré with its alluvial silt.

Within a couple of hours we'd reached the concrete capped well at Tiririne and began heading into the broken sandstone country of the Tassili-Hoggar which characterised the rest of our trip to Tamanrasset. As far as I can now divine we were moving up the Oued Tagant, stopping at lunch time at its well, hemmed in a narrow sandy gorge. A group of dark-skinned Tuareg women in indigo robes were camped there and rather to our surprise, enthusiastically began peddling a selection of silver jewellery and leather crafts instead of remaining quiet, dignified and slightly scornful as our preconceptions would have preferred. Their hard sell was all the more bizarre as they were the only people we saw for three days. No one bought anything and the flies drawn to the animal dung found around all desert wells also made the lunch break tiresome. We were glad to move on.

The gorge closed in still further until we came out onto

a rocky plateau with another line of hills on the horizon. Chadli pointed out some tough, gnarled cypress wood which he advised burned especially well and recommended we all stock up for the evening. When that time came we set ourselves down in a gallery of strangely weathered outcrops set among deep banks of sand. One unusual mushroom-like formation, which doubtless appears in some picture book somewhere, supported a huge bulb of rock as big as a room perched on two eroded pedestals no bigger than a dustbin.

Mark found himself an empty bottle of Jonnie Walker and filled it with Saharan sand as a souvenir while Mike tore off on his bike to resolve some recondite strop or other, possibly frustrated at the rather tame follow-the-leader pace which left little opportunity for larking around or gunning it. Clive managed to get the Swiss couple talking that night. They too possibly felt a little out of touch on Anna's southern tour but seemed to be quietly enjoying themselves and were less wary of us now that the van had a string of successful starts behind it. Dalek set up a tripod on a dune to capture the sunset and presently Mike returned for dinner, glanced up at Dalek and observed dryly, 'How crepuscular.'

The following day saw us crossing another broad flood plain dotted with occasional trees and small dunes. To make riding more interesting, Mark rode along thee low sand hills, making the occasional airborne excursion from hump to hump. As his confidence grew he speeded up and left the van behind.

The van. For some reason it was overheating again, even with the electric fan going full blast. A quick look under the cowling explained why. Water, or to be precise steam, was venting from a broken seam in one of the radiator joints and broiling my already comfortably warm right leg. Topping up with a bottle of Rad-o-Plug, we rolled back the cab's canvas roof and revelled in the breeze. With a jerrican of water handy and an eye on the temporarily tranquillised temperature gauge, we sped along to catch up

Up ahead Pete was waving furiously.

'Mark's had an accident, he's over there. I think he's alright but he hasn't moved yet.'

I drew the van round onto the hard gravel where Mark lay curled up next to his prostrate bike and my heart rose to my mouth.

Mike was tending to him. He'd performed a similar stunt to Bob, only at twice the height and three times the speed. Seeing the unavoidable drop-off Mark had instinctively slowed down, the worst thing to do, and at the last second accelerated off the dune's edge crash landing the bike hard on the gravel. As we stood around wondering what to do Mark suddenly got up, a little winded and bendy legged but with nothing broken. His split-second reaction had probably saved a much worse injury. Slowing down, a rider is pitched over the bars ahead of the tumbling bike which often as not falls on the rider – as Jonny had found out in Egypt

Shocked but otherwise OK, Mark limped over to the van and hoisted himself in while I got on his bike. It too seemed to have come away from the landing intact, a little bent but rideable.

I followed the van cautiously, remembering how I'd anticipated accidents like Bob's and Mark's when planning the trip months earlier, knowing even then that reckless riding, though unavoidable, would be the single biggest danger of this type of tour. It would have been unrealistic to expect adventure-seeking bikers to be as mindful and vigilant as I'd become following years of hard-won desert experience. New to the desert and used to the tedious frustrations of road-riding, they were bound to cut loose at the sight of the Sahara's infinite expanses, ignorant of its particular dangers and mollified by the presence of the van. Furthermore, having a leader to follow meant they could engage less brain power than normal – a danger I'd learned to be wary of as a teenage rock climber. When you're leading a pitch you concentrate fully, judging your moves shrewdly and so climbing at your best. Seconding is of course much safer and exerts merely physical and not psychological demands; slap-dash moves will suffice as the consequence is only a minor fall. So it was in the desert. Mike especially rode with an occasional brain-out recklessness and yet he was the only one who completed the whole trip.

Later, following some stop or another, Mark's bike refused to start and I was left kick-kick-kicking until someone noticed I was missing and came back. Despite some protracted and ingenious bodging of the lifeless electrics, the Suzuki never regained consciousness and we strapped it onto the towing device where it stayed all the way to Marseille.

So this left Pete and Mike, who were busy developing a mutual if never-to-be-consummated enmity, now flying the tattered remnants of A Trip Of A Lifetime's banner. Perhaps I should have called it A Trip To End A Lifetime.

The Cathedral

L ater that afternoon we pulled up for lunch in a broad valley speckled with thorny acacia trees. A few minutes earlier Chadli had said this was a place where gazelles were frequently spotted and, although the only large mammals I'd ever seen in the desert other than humans were camels, just before we stopped the lithe tan figure of a startled Dorcas gazelle had raced across the desert floor and out of sight. Either the keen-eyed Chadli had slyly spotted it and presaged its appearance or he knew his area better than we'd ever credited.

Our convoy stopped by a couple of trees, and piste-weary figures emerged from the vehicles to stretch their legs. Parking up in the wilderness by some kind of marker seems to be an indelible human instinct and on hot days it's a temptation to drive right into the shade of a thorn tree. As I'd learned to my cost, that's something you only do once – the penalty being a tyreful of thorn tips which work themselves into the rubber and produce multiple punctures for days to come.

Over lunch Mark, seemingly recovered from his fall and desperate to get riding again, fiddled about with his bike's wiring. Tantalised by weak and erratic sparks from the spark plug, he was sure it was just an obscure electrical connection loosened by the crash. Fix it and he'd be riding

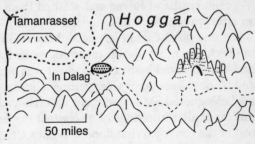

again instead of sitting in awkward silence in the back of Anna's plushly-sprung Land Cruiser. He swung away at the starter, causing the odd, muffled bark to pop from the end of the silencer, but nothing set the engine ablaze. Meanwhile Clive had come up with an innovative remedy for the van's leaking radiator. My stories of obsolete lorries running in the central African jungles on hardwood pistons and bamboo suspension had got him thinking that nature's bounty held the solution to all mechanical woes. He wandered around a likely-looking oued with Dalek, searching for some fine clay with which to seal off the leak. It was a nice try but lasted only as long as the next set of corrugations. Meanwhile Mark's frantic tinkerings seemed to have extended beyond the time cordially allocated for such things and when impatient murmurs from the others reached his ears he was reluctantly obliged to give up and we got moving again.

The piste became sandier and more convoluted as we moved closer into the narrowing valleys radiating from the Hoggar. Any notions I was having of trying to memorise this run for another time were muddled into a jumble of confusing short-cuts taken in all directions. Occasionally Dalek would drive his mother's car. Winding down the window, he'd set the cruise control and sit out on the sill, holding onto the roof rack, reaching down to steer with his other hand. It was a novel driving technique I'd not come across before and something worth adopting in the sweaty din of the 101's cab. In the end we removed the doors of the Meccano-era Land Rover and stashed them in the back in an effort to cool the van's interior.

At one point Chadli left us and drove off in Anna's car to check the route ahead, returning with the news that it had been blocked by recent floods. It was our third day out and by now some of us were getting a little weary, although the beleaguered SMT contingent was relieved at having got this far at all. Mutterings of discontent rippled through the rest of the convoy. What floods? What's Chadli playing at?

Bloody guides. For another hour we drove around haphazardly over low passes and up slithering banks of sand looking for a suitable place to camp out of the wind. Eventually a flat and sheltered spot was found. And what a place! Cathedral Camp we called it. Behind us a massive spire of rock like melted wax rose over our encampment, replicating Barcelona's famous Church of the Holy Family but without the century-old scaffolding. There was even a huge central portal adding to the ecclesiastical effect, although it was stranded halfway up the face. The three tired parties picked themselves a spot and set about their chores, letting the tension of a long day's driving ease away with the spreading shadows. It wasn't until a couple of years later that I realised that Cathedral Camp was only a few miles from the well at Tadjenout where Colonel Flatters and most of his company had met their predictable doom in 1881.

Chadli decided to do a spot of traditional baking that evening. Stoking up a small fire until it had reduced itself to embers, he pushed away the glowing coals, scooped out a pit in the hot sand and poured in a thick doughy mixture of flour and water. This he carefully re-covered with sand and the embers and left to cook. Half an hour later he exhumed a perfectly baked soda bread bap. Patting off the sand, he broke off a piece and passed the rest around. It would be nice to record that the warm chunks of bread baked for us by a Chaamba tribesman in the sands of the Sahara were as delicious as they were romantic. But this particular example of bush cuisine was disappointing, an insipid and dense fusion of flour and water on which we chewed intently while mouthing polite "mmmm"s.

It's often observed that the best time in the desert is the end of the day, when you can appreciate the mellower aspect of its Promethean presence. The heat subsides and very often the wind with it, taking away the stresses of the day's travel. The only sound is the contented murmur of people around the crackling of a fire while overhead, moonless nights unroll a dense carpet of stars across the heavens. There's only one constellation I know up there and I call it the North Pointer. Some of it is part of Orion or Orion's Belt but, lacking a sufficiently fertile astrological imagination, to me it's always represented a large right-angled arrow head with a tiny tail, that's visible from early evening to the middle of the night and points, most useful-ly, just west of north. I first spotted it while sleeping beneath the bleached limestone cliffs near Cassis, just east of Marseille when setting out on my first desert trip and since then it's remained a familiar friend in the night skies, always pointing home.

The following morning Chadli led us on foot to some pre-historic engravings close to the camp which bordered the broad valley of Tin Tarabine. With muscles, poise and curiosity stupored from too much butt-numbing driving, we stumbled around lethargically while Chadli hopped nimbly from rock to rock, hands set behind his back like a visiting Royal. Occasionally he'd flick out a hand, pointing to a nearby rock wall, but was clearly unwilling to get bogged down in tedious anthropological explanations. We'd scurry up to find some doubtless ancient but hardly stirring outlines of anonymous ruminants a few inches high. These were mere bus shelter scrawlings but the fact that they were everywhere, that people had once hunted and grazed their bovine herds around this dramatic but now arid setting brought the place alive. You could imagine the waters of the Tin Tarabine meandering through the grassy valley and some straw-chewing cowherd idling away his siesta with a rock-side doodle.

Later on Chadli stopped at another site where the piste squeezed through a narrow canyon blocked by small dunes. For once the 101, lightened by gallons of consumed fuel, clambered through effortlessly while the others got stuck. Here the slabs of dark grey stone were engraved with geometric hieroglyphs, the unique *tifinar* script of the Tuareg's *tamachek* language, said to resemble the ancient

Libyan Script, whatever that is.

Having spent the last two days cutting across the Hoggar's radial drainage channels, we now turned northwest and followed a narrowing valley "upstream" into the mountains. We passed the shrivelled remains of a camel, reduced to a shrunken parchment of thick hide around a frame of bones. The agonies of death had contorted the beast's backbone, arching its head close to its rump as it kicked itself into a low bowl of sand which still encircled it.

Mid-afternoon saw the valley narrow into a stream bed and ahead of us loomed a seemingly impenetrable wall. The piste became confined by low outcrops and began twisting and rolling as we climbed up into the highlands across sandy oueds and through vehicle-wide clefts. At one point we came upon a large Italian camper van, its chubby white-haired driver and his wife clearly not intent on slipping gently into their autumn years. He cheerfully probed Chadli about the route ahead and together they hunkered down over a sand map to clarify the Southern Piste's finer navigational nuances. The thought of trying to retrace our complex route back to Djanet without Chadli seemed impossible, but with directions memorised and a *bon voyage*, the Italian van headed east across our still warm tracks.

As the day drew to an end we rejoined the peripheries of civilisation, pausing at the *zeriba* village of In Dalag where the uninhibited kids crowded round as we drew some water from their well. For many Saharan travellers, the act of drawing well water represents an significant facet of desert travel, forging a brief connection with the vital resource whose very scarcity defines the desert. It makes you feel that you're really Out There, living off your wits and acting out an age-old human task, instead of just skimming over the ostensibly hostile land on more prosaically acquired town tap water.

Every village will have a well and all long established routes will have sources every 200 miles or so. The Michelin

953 map marks many wells in the Sahara with handy tips such as *forage artésien (sulfureuse)*, or *eau bonne, trés abondante*; or else warning *eau bonne à 8m, puits dangereux*, or *eau mauvaise*. On most ordinary pistes it's rare to depend on wells, which are often hard to locate on the first attempt; instead most travellers fill up at a reliable pumped source in the town, carrying enough water to get to the next town. In the French colonial era many wells were ringed with concrete walls to keep out sand and dying animals. Village wells that were used frequently to irrigate gardens or palmeries might have a crude pulley system fashioned from forked tree trunks and a wheeled beam; these are gradually being replaced with diesel or solar-powered pumps.

Tap-trained squeamishness is soon overcome once you realise that most well-water tastes better than anything you're fed at home, although common hygienic sense needs to be applied to remote and rarely used wells. Any locals present will often look on pityingly as you struggle to flip and sink the old tin can or knotted inner tube which act as buckets. Or else they'll insist that the incompetent passer by stand to one side as they lean over the well, elbow on one knee, expertly flipping the container and swiftly drawing it up in a few strokes using the full height of their upwardly stretched arm. Water drawn like this is very rarely paid for, although a well-keeper might be tipped for his trouble.

As the Michelin's descriptions suggest, ground water is subject to various mineral influences, not all of them palatable, though only chloride-tainted water from the lowest sandy basins is deadly to humans in the long run. Dying animals falling into a well are much more ruinous and will soon render the water undrinkable. The well at the famous Arbre du Ténéré in Niger, one of only two sources on the 450-mile Agadez–Bilma caravan route, became polluted in this way: the replacement well is little better and is classed as *trés mauvaise* at over 130 feet. The eponymous tree itself was once a legendary and vital landmark, the only tree in

an area the size of France. It was knocked down by a reversing lorry in the early Seventies (or so the most enduring
story goes) and is now displayed in the museum at Niamey.

Leaving the village and well of In Dalag along a rutted piste
of soft sand which left the slow-moving bikes struggling to
stay upright, we rejoined what I soon realised was the
"outer ring road" encompassing the Atakor – the dramatic
central massif of the Hoggar mountains. From here I recognised the way back to Tamanrasset, 45 miles away and next
morning, as the other two vehicles went with Clive and
Mike to a reputedly notable cascade, I returned directly to
Tam with Pete, Mark and the ailing van. Saying goodbye to
Anna and Chadli, I took a note of our guide's address while
Anna generously offered me her card should I ever be passing through Algiers.

Relieved to be at the head of my own one-van convoy
once more, I rumbled along the corrugated piste towards
Tam with Pete riding alongside. Within an hour I spotted
the familiar profile of Hadrianne, the table mountain visible
from Tamanrasset's southern limits, and soon after we
joined the trans-Saharan Highway a few miles south of
Tam. We'd reached the end of our four day off-road excursion from Djanet. I felt the usual mixture of relief – a
chance to take a breather – allied with a twinge of regret
that we were back in the predictable confines of the normal
world. Pete meanwhile dropped to his knees and offered a
papal benediction to the blacktop he'd so dearly missed.

To the Land of Terror

At Tamanrasset the five of us welcomed the change to a slacker routine, with spare time to clean up, wander around looking at other people or service our machines, before going through it all again. Anna and the Swiss couple were heading back north and so was Pete, the only one of us with a proper job awaiting his return. He left in the company of a couple of German bikers for the four-day ride to Algiers, running ahead of the pitiless Grim Reaper who'd been stalking our tour and who, in Pete's words, "tended to lay down his scythe and start up his chain saw."

With only Mike left riding a bike (Mark having unsuccessfully scoured Tam's bush mechanics for a bike-resuscitating component), the group was now a pale spectre of the original tour. No one was in a rush to get back and when we ran into Swiss Steve and Caroline still on their way to Guinea we decided to accompany them to the Mali frontier at Bordj Moktar, 350 miles southwest of Tam, instead of heading back to HbG via Amguid as we'd planned. From Bordj we could head north up the more desolate of the two trans–Saharan pistes, the so-called Tanez-

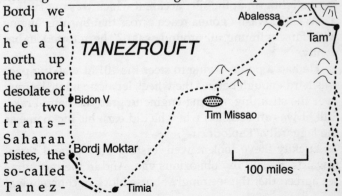

rouft. Furthermore I was pleased to re-encounter Steve who seemed a like-minded Saharan who knew his pistes from his elbow and with whom I might travel in the future.

With the 101 repaired and fuelled up, and the defunct Suzuki trailing from the carrier like a lifeboat, Steve, Caroline and the four of us were ready to set off for Bordj. As far as we knew, the turn-off to the west was located around 25 miles north of Tam just after the village of Tit. However turn-offs are rarely patently clear in the desert: a sign promising "Bordj Moktar this way" is unusual, it's as likely to be a robust concrete block whose faded lettering is obscured by a riot of graffiti. We pulled up off the road at one such block, wanting to be certain before heading off blindly into the west along the mass of promising tracks.

I hopped out of the van, at that time running without its engine cowling so that we could keep an eye on the re-braised radiator, to confer with Steve. As we scrutinised his map laid out on the bonnet, I caught sight of the van rolling slowly forwards towards the back of his Toyota. Clive sat helpless in the passenger seat, unable to stem the accumulated three tons of van from butting its flat nose into the Cruiser's behind. The result was a clean but indelible dent in the back door of Steve's prized car.

'Why didn't you do something?' I beseeched Clive, hiding a slight grin at the silly accident which was my fault.

'What? I wasn't gonna reach across that burning engine with fans spinning all around was I?' he retorted indignantly.

He had a point. Trying to steer the 101 at walking pace was hard enough behind the wheel, let alone while leaning over the steaming, rattling engine to grab the hand brake. Still, it was an occasion when he did earn his nickname as the laggardly "Diplodocus".

Luckily Steve took it well, casting only a mild threat towards me and my obnoxious van. And in the meantime we agreed that the seemingly obtuse block of concrete was in fact a significant marker and so we turned towards it and into the afternoon sun.

It was near Tit in 1902 that the French scraped through a decisive and final battle against the Ahaggar Tuareg, the last and most fierce of the Tuareg clans to surrender to French control. A bloody afternoon of fighting with a French patrol sent out from In Salah to punish one Tuareg transgression too many ended in the slaying of 150 of the Ahaggar's finest warriors. As René Lecler described in *Sahara:*, his sometimes fanciful 1954 account of selected Saharan histories

> In the space of a few hours and in the heart of their hitherto inviolate homeland, the myth of the blue warriors' invincibility, carefully built up through centuries of hard fighting and clever politics, had been smashed to smithereens...the Hoggar [Ahaggar], proudest of all the Tuareg, had been beaten into submission.

From the village of Tit a well defined corrugated track led onto the flat plain which eventually spread out into the featureless *reg* (gravel plain) of the Tanezrouft. Within an hour we'd passed the collection of villages and irrigated allotments known as Abalessa, which gives me another opportunity to deviate from the adventures of our advancing convoy and to briefly relate one more historically interesting Saharan anecdote.

In 1925, French archaeologists unearthed a tomb near Abalessa which seemed to lend tangible credibility to the local Tuareg legend of Tin Hinan, the Ahaggar's ancestral queen – an especially significant find as Abalessa also happens to be the Ahaggar Tuareg's capital, and the home of their *amenoukal*. According to the Tuareg, Tin Hinan was exiled from the Berber lands of Morocco and on arriving here begat their race. Some say that it was her aloofness and noble demeanour which gave the Ahaggar their name and striking disposition. Artefacts recovered from the tomb, which dates from the sixth century, certainly suggested a regal female personage, and some items linked her with the Roman era – a period which predates the Tuareg arrival in the area. That she is the "mother" of the matrilineal Tuareg has recently been confirmed as a politically motivated myth dreamt up by the Tuareg just a few hundred years ago. It nevertheless corresponds nicely with the Tuareg's decidedly un-Islamic and even chivalric respect for their women who, unlike the men, go about unveiled. The latest debunking of this folk myth now even casts doubt on Tin Hinan's sex, although the mysterious person was certainly of Caucasian descent.

Still, no time for archeological investigations on this trip, we had a piste to cross. A maddeningly corrugated track carried us to the last Hoggar village of Silet where a checkout with the police was mandatory, there being no settlements for the next 300 miles. A short distance west of the village the piste passed through a gap in the isolated outcrop of Adrar Isket and from here we followed the thinly vegetated line which defines the Oued Tamanrasset. The piste from this point was marked every few kilometres with prominent orange and white oil drums set atop plinths of dirt, something the much more frequented and virtually unmarked trans–Saharan Highway south of Tam could definitely do with.

Our destination that night was the well of Tim Missao, tucked away inside a narrow canyon about 120 miles from Silet, but it wasn't till the following afternoon that we spotted the derelict stone hut and the twin-buttressed rocks which led to the gorge mouth. It took some scrambling around a few dead ends of a hidden valley before a small dune led us into the sandy canyon and the well. The brittle remains of beasts abandoned by a departing encampment added a grisly edge and a noisome drone of flies disturbed an otherwise tranquil setting, but it was nevertheless a good place to spend the night. Now well out of the highlands of the Tassili and the Hoggar, the temperature had increased noticeably and the ever impetuous Mike, who'd found relief in riding without a helmet, was already lying prone in the shade, suffering from a light dose of sunstroke.

Graffiti both ancient and contemporary covers the gorge walls around Tim Missao and there's said to be a lot more in the vicinity, including some significant prehistoric depictions documented by Lhote in the 1950s. The most interesting of his finds show horse-drawn chariots of the type associated with the Libyan Garamanteans – further evidence that chariots had once crossed a less arid Sahara. Back at Tim Missao with Swiss Steve a year later I went looking for these unusual paintings, but my vague directions led me nowhere in particular. I was however rewarded with a rather fine Neolithic treasure: half of a well-worn grinding stone on which grass seeds would have been mashed with an ovoid pestle. To Steve's prosaic eye it was just a boring bit of rock. For me though, it symbolised my dwindling preoccupation with simplistic "piste bashing" and an unfolding polarisation of our Saharan aspirations which was to prematurely terminate our travels within a week or so.

But back to the SMT camp, the more lethargic among us clung like bats to the narrowing shade of the gorge walls, wrapped up against the tiresome flies, while others wandered off up the ravine. A truckful of soldiers, one of the many units which patrol this presumably sensitive but improbably vast southern border, stopped at the well to have a quick wash and then moved on. Near Adrar Isket we'd been checked over by a rather hostile armed unit, though what we could have been up to other then simple-minded tourism was anybody's guess. That evening no one was very hungry and without the bundlesome tomfoolery of the early days, we slipped away to our beds.

At the stone hut next morning, and with a still poorly Mike

laid out in the back of Steve's Toyota, the piste forked with the orange drums leading directly westwards to Bordj, a quicker but forbidden piste. With some difficulty we found the markers for the permitted route: small concrete bollards ticking off the approach of Timiaouine (or "Timia") in ten-kilometre increments. The country we drove through was flat and sandy with the odd sprig of vegetation and ripple of relief; the Tanezrouft would be flatter and sandier still and totally barren.

Having read several deserty travel books, I can't recall one that satisfactorily describes the appearance of the desert wilderness. This is in part because the daytime desert is far less dramatic than many writers (and photographers) would have you believe. For the most part, its sun-blasted contours are drab, or at worst plain bleak, an uninspiring composition in grey and ochre that leaves little for the imagination to play with. The Great Basin Desert of the southwest US is far more dramatic by comparison. Only at the end of the day does it take on a magical aura, coloured by the long shadows and the ruddy tones of a setting sun. The pale, washed-out yellows become enriched oranges and reds while the enlongating shadows expose the infinite curves of the dunes.

Once on the southern Tanezrouft I spotted some flat rocks which gave off an indubitably lilac phosphorescence, but I'm sure it was an ultra-violet oddity of the unfolding dusk. Naturally I've encountered beautiful and dramatic patches of desert: the Illizi–Djanet run, the dunes north of El Golea and those south of In Salah, Assekrem, but I've also ridden all day through forlorn vistas that resemble nothing so much as a vast bulldozed building site of heaped rubble and sand.

What is much more interesting of course is how an individual responds to all this wilderness and here I've read some understandably mystically-tinged and introspective accounts that come close to explaining the desert's singular appeal. Usually they boil down to a portentous reminder of one's insignificance in the humbling presence of infinite creation. This example by Margaret Hubbard from *The Rough Guide to Morocco* is pretty definitive*:

> I can find no terms that will sufficiently describe the effect the desert had on me. It was awesome and inspiring and it silenced me. I also found that the more recent preoccupations that I had about my life, work, and relationships had entirely slipped from my mind. Yet strangely, I could recall with absolute clarity images from over ten years ago. I remain convinced that the desert, with its simplicity, its expansiveness, and its power changed me in some way.

This reaction is subtly different to the feelings inspired by the unbroken monotony of the ocean or the breathtaking grandeur of the mountains, both similarly compelling environments. But travelling through all these wild places you experience the spellbinding silence beneath the hum of the wind, the unattainable horizons which surround you and the rare thrill of self sufficiency, of being in control of your destiny. It's an intoxicating combination in which danger plays a pervasive, but not dominant, role. For these reasons (and innumerable others, which I gave up trying to work out ages ago), the desert is an easy place for me to feel good in. If you must have it encapsulated in a single word then that word is freedom. Freedom from, and freedom to.

With Mike off sick, Mark was delighted with the chance to be back on a bike, and the six of us checked off the bollards' withering mileages as the vegetation thickened perceptibly towards Timia, giving a false impression that we had reached the sub-Saharan Sahel. We spent the night in a dune-sheltered building site where some of us mysteriously threw up and by next afternoon, having passed through the humble mud brick village of Timiaouine, smartened ourselves up to enter the notorious outpost of Bordj Badji Moktar.

To be stationed at a sterile town like Bordj, halfway point on the Tanezrouft piste, can't do a lot for your sense of humour and is it any wonder when a cocky traveller tiring of the onerous demands of yet another African frontier rubs a heat-struck official up the wrong way? Personally I approach every border as if I'm going to be there for days, expecting either to have to bribe my way into the country or to be turned back for some petty irregularity. This is the way it works in Africa; it's tedious and it's slow but it's the same for everyone. In my experience they don't just pick on tourists because we're rich Euros, we must first prove to be arrogant or otherwise dysfunctional rich Euros before we get The Treatment.

Luckily we didn't have anything to fear as we were staying in the country and heading north, but even Steve and Caroline passed through the rigmarole without undue delay and were set free to proceed directly to Tessalit, the Mali frontier post a hundred miles to the south.

By 1992 things were not so rosy at Bordj Moktar. Officials there took advantage of the Tuareg disturbances and having just discharged a southbound party, dashed into a set of Tuareg outfits and robbed them with uncommon violence and brutality. They were recognised by the survivors, but such a vicious attack, and many similar recent events in once-peaceful Algeria are the very worst cases that travelling in Africa can offer. They settle into the sensational mythology of the Dark Continent like that of some dreaded urban Front Line; "Africa? Oo-er, I wouldn't go there if I were you."

Saying goodbye to Steve and Caroline, we left the Tanezrouft's now sweltering core and headed northwards into the void. Variously translated from the Arabic as "The Land of Terror, Thirst, Evil or Emptiness" (the Arabic equivalent of the Tuareg Ténéré), the Tanezrouft piste runs over 850 miles from the tarmac's end at Reggane in central Algeria down to Gao on the Niger river in eastern Mali. Flat as the proverbial hedgehog's air bed in its northern half, this is where the side-splitting Saharan simile "like a beach with the tide gone out, forever" fits nicely.

Until Algeria closed down in the early Nineties the Tanezrouft was a relatively well-frequented route, favoured in particular by European entrepreneurs keen to flog clapped-out Peugeots and the like to car-starved West Africa. You can still find these vehicles south of the Sahara, invariably crammed with passengers to the point of reckless intimacy and driven to ruin as part of the extensive bush taxi network.

At best the car-trade business (still surviving today along the West Coast route) was a mildly lucrative sideline for semi-professional itinerants who knew what sort of vehicles and components were needed and had reliable contacts in the West African capitals. They'd gather a bunch of mates and drive down some cars, an old bus loaded with more engines and body parts and maybe a 4WD to help out in the frequent boggings. They knew the pitfalls of the crossing, what was needed to accomplish it and also what merchandise to bring back and sell in Europe. In its way the Tanezrouft was still a vital desert trade route for their commerce and the sub-Saharan dealers knew the exact value of what they were buying.

At the other extreme might be a band of wily students who'd heard that driving a brace of Peugeot 504s down the Tanezrouft, selling them in Ouagadougou, and then chilling out on the beach in Togo was a canny scam. People down there would buy anything that ran, and would pay good money, certainly enough to pay for a Gold Coast suntan, some trinkets and a flight home. They'd track down the cheapest *cinq cent quatre* they could find and without so much as a reflective warning triangle set off to cross the Sahara in their summer hols, the worst time of year when each person consumed up to two gallons of water daily and disorientating sandstorms blew for days.

Like most first-timers, they underrated the Sahara,

assuming it to be a bigger than average wilderness with an over-romanticised "Beau Geste" mystique which simply required a little more driving than normal. Many of the wrecks which lie abandoned along the major pistes started life as part of just such a trip: poorly prepared and over-loaded vehicles which were left to be picked clean by passing truckers. Some such enterprises ended in nothing short of tragedy, like a sortie involving three young Germans, each driving their own car, who became lost in a summer sandstorm. With experience, any Saharan knows that it's essential to stop and wait in any situation on the piste when visibility is lost. This is when the seemingly excessive reserves of water you're compelled to carry become absolutely vital. The three Germans were stumbled upon three months later; way off piste, they'd drunk every fluid they could find before scrawling farewell notes to their families back home.

Around fifteen years ago the entire Algerian section of the Tanezrouft was marked out every two kilometres with ten-metre high solar beacons. Batteries would store up the day's solar charge to flash it away overnight, enabling the featureless route to be traversed safely in the cool of the night – something that piste-wise truckers are apt do. But vandalism, theft and malfunction have since taken their toll so that when we passed through not one of them worked, though the surviving poles remained very useful route markers by day. There are two other significant landmarks and no wells in the 420 miles to Reggane where the tarmac resumes, but otherwise the Tanezrouft is about as perfectly blank a place as nature can devise. Occasional sandy patches give you something to think about, but perhaps the biggest danger is not running into the defunct beacons.

The pressing heat brought about a feeling of lethargy and anti-climax as our tour dribbled towards its inescapable finale. The ever destructive corrugations, surely the terrestrial manifestation of the wicked *djenouns* had again fractured the radiator, making it a good 20°C hotter inside the cramped cab than out. The doors were off, the cab roof was rolled back, the back flap rolled up, and the engine cowling was in the back; short of blowing on the engine, we were giving the cantankerous York motor all the draught we could muster. In return it remonstrated with a head-splitting din that only a diesel can contrive and made all the metal surfaces around too hot too touch. Whoever was driving latched onto their ear defenders, edged as far from the engine as possible without falling out and stoically steered the van past the solar poles, car wrecks and other stark remnants of human endeavour.

We passed the historic ruins of Bidon V, the Fifth Oil Drum dropped off by a trailblazing expedition half a century ago which is now something of an obsolete focal point along the Tanezrouft. Wind-battered hangars and miscellaneous bits of skewed metal litter the site where once mail planes would land to refuel, guided in by a long-dead light beacon. During the French colonial era, water tanks were maintained every 200 kilometres along the Tanezrouft and after aviation technology rendered its airstrip redundant, Bidon Cinq became one such watering hole where fuel was also sometimes available. A well-worn legend tells of a short-sighted warden stationed alone at the depot who sold the last of his water to an insistent party and who was found dead a few days later.

Some 200 miles north of Bordj we selected a likely looking pole and with immense relief I turned off the engine and let the van coast to a halt. Peeling away the ear defenders, I stumbled out of the cab and tried to shake away the incessant intracranial ringing.

Cracking Up

Do you think it's a good idea sleeping right on the track? I heard Mike's appeal. 'Don't you think we should move off it a bit?'

'Nah, it'll be alright, they're not going to drive right by the beacon are they,' I sighed, too weary to figure out a better place. There was as much chance of us getting run down anywhere around here, I reasoned, assuming that, as on the Hoggar route, the trucks found their own way through the night. But something was bugging Mike, who'd been in a heat-struck strop for the last couple of days, and unfortunately that something was me. Within a few minutes some other petty decision enraged him and, grabbing a couple of firewood planks, he lashed them together into a crude crucifix, stormed off into the dark and stabbed them into the ground.

'There you go,' he said acidly, strutting back to the camp. I wandered over and read the sarcastic epitaph on my mock-tombstone with a chuckle, taking it in the prankish spirit with which I presumed it had been planted. But my genuinely lighthearted response was not appreciated and a trio of sullen faces averted themselves from my grin as I walked back.

Oh dear, the proverbial lead balloon had dropped with a heavy thud, abruptly souring the mood. Even Clive and the ever cheerful Mark seemed to have turned against me. A clammy unease settled over the rest of that evening. I put it down to the day's heat and the unsettling agoraphobic expanse around us, both of whose effects on human behaviour are well known. But was some deep-rooted dissatisfaction with the Skipper also emerging – had familiarity festered into contempt? At times in those final days I had the disturbing certainty that the three of them were going to gang up on me and beat me to a pulp. I even felt a tautness across my back from where I expected the blows to come. Perhaps the Land of Terror was getting to us all.

That night a *truck* did indeed pass close by, briefly waking us all. As its approach had been incorporated into whatever I was dreaming prior to waking, I innocently enquired next morning how the noise had manifested itself in everyone else's dreams.

'Oh how did the truck come through in *your* dream?' sneered Mike acidly, delighted that his doubt over our overnight positioning had been vindicated. Well it had come by, but it had hardly swerved at the last minute; it was probably just checking we were alright or if there was anything worth stealing. And now there was more animosity towards my reluctance to remove one of the van's windscreen panes to get more air flowing through the cab. Sitting in the van was certainly uncomfortable but with every northern mile the temperature was cooling off and soon we could re-cover the deafening engine. Nevertheless I recognised that perhaps I'd better acquiesce on this one and unscrewed the fragile glass which sure enough ended up cracked.

The chillingly isolating feeling of being the helpless Fatty (or was it Speckie?) in *Lord of the Flies*, unfairly reviled and unable to escape, gradually faded as the marginally cooler day released our tensions. Unavoidable interpersonal weariness, the bland dregs of our remaining food supplies and the anticlimactic end of the trip were all taking their toll on morale. But there'd been no earlier dissent and within a day or two the heaviness was forgotten and Mark magnanimously apologised – about that evening I'd presumed, though he was in fact referring to some other occasion which I'd not even noticed.

Around midday we came across a motionless vehicle – an old German Hanomag truck, the sort of thing the Post Office might have used to erect telegraph poles across the Scottish moors in the mid-Fifties. Its German occupants, a slim young woman and a smaller older man were glad to see us.

'*Ça va?*' I offered the *pistard's* customary greeting.

They both spoke English and the driver, Werner pointed out a fractured exhaust pipe which I offered to fix. As I dug out our tools from the back of the van it became evident that they too seemed to be suffering from a mutual strain. His partner Ingrid's eyes had widened at the appearance of some long overdue Real Men whose part-dismantled vehicle towing a lame bike looked like it'd had seen the wars. While I undertook the surprisingly simple repair, Clive and Mike turned towards Ingrid, smarmy side up, while Werner peered under his truck, studiously admiring my handiwork.

They too were coming to the end of a long tour, having been across the Ténéré studying Tuareg customs and myths and collecting their artefacts. Werner was attached to Bonn University and the trip had something to do with a thesis of his. Ingrid, it seemed, had come along for the ride and appeared to have had enough of the wishy-washy Werner and the hot and boring desert. Hearing where they'd been, it seemed all the more odd that Werner had been flummoxed by such a straightforward fault in what was after all a 30-year-old vehicle.

As I emerged from under the Hanomag, Ingrid, cigarette cocked, turned her fulsome gaze on me with a "Gee, you're so clever, how d'you do it" look which seemed to be saying it might be *his* truck but *I* do what I want. She got more of a reaction from Clive and Mike who'd by now entered a low scale contest for her attentions while the shaky Werner babbled away with me about deserty things and Mark kicked about in the sand.

Something was up between the two of them but it was agreed we'd camp together that night further up the track if the Hanomag – one of those rare vehicles that was slower than the 101 – could make it. The evening indeed saw us encamped protectively in the still unchanged void, but now with a revised set of group dynamics for which, after the previous night, I should have been grateful. Ingrid focused purposefully on the charming duo with wide-eyed observations like "Mmmm, is that *real* leather?" at which the feckless Werner twitched and shrank. I, meanwhile, focused my attention on Werner: though I felt sorry for him, I was also genuinely interested in his travels in the Ténéré. I was particularly impressed by his 1:200,000 IGN maps, never having seen one before, and he proudly showed me a sheet titled something like "Erg Capot Rey" which covered a one-thousand-square-kilometre patch of the northern Ténéré. Apart from a couple of spot heights and some squiggles representing dunes, the pale yellow square was utterly blank. He also hauled out some Tuareg regalia which he'd bought off an impoverished clansman: a rather stiff looking camel saddle with its distinctive three-pronged pommel and an impressive but cumbersome broad sword which a Targui traditionally wore. I myself had bought a natty little dagger from a Targui who'd appeared from out of the blue, as they have the knack of doing, between Timia and Bordj. Though crudely cast it boasted some fine detail which set it apart from the average Stanley knife.

We rejoined the other four who'd by now become subdued and, seizing the initiative, Werner cracked open a half-bottle of the seemingly ubiquitous JW he'd managed to slip through at Bordj Moktar. None of us had particularly missed drinking in alcohol-free Algeria and I myself could-

n't stomach the stuff, but soon the entertainingly resource-
ful Clive proposed a drinking game called "Sevens", the
idea being simply to count backwards from a hundred,
missing out numbers which included or were multiples of
seven. The real fun with Sevens lay in the forfeit for every
mistake: a slug of whisky.

Inevitably – and essentially for the game's enjoyment –
the swift sober reductions were eventually muddled and
soon the four of them (Ingrid and I abstained) were having
difficulty counting back any numbers, let alone missing out
the forbidden multiples. Werner proved to be less mathe-
matically agile than most.

'94, 93, 92, 91, ninety…, Schisse!'

'Shaaaizerrr!!' the other three mimicked as the hapless
Werner gulped back another shot. Ingrid looked on in
unqualified disgust. Soon he was utterly incapable of omit-
ting even the easy inclusive numbers

'100, 98, 97 – Ahh Schisse!'

'SHAAAIZERRR!!' they roared.

By now even Mark, Clive and Mike were having trouble
getting beyond the eighties and the glass was merely being
filled, drained and passed on.

While they worked their way to the bottom of the bottle
I went off for a quiet contemplation of the stars as this
would be our last night on the piste, the real desert. From
the slurring group I could just hear the complex subtrac-
tions punctuated with the ever more frequent and forceful
refrain "Argh Schisse!... SHAAAIZZERRR!!!".

Next morning a part-bleary bunch headed north towards
Reggane and the end of the piste. We passed the derelict
outpost of Poste Weygand where a water tank supplied
trans-Tanezrouft traffic and where a small garden was
being tended by some enterprising squatter. To the east a
track led to the ruins of Ouallen where the French used to
experiment with atmospheric nuclear blasts before the
Pacific atolls were deemed more suitable.

One last patch of soft sand, a final dune and the Tanezrouft came to an end at the "port" of Reggane. Reporting our safe arrival to the police, we were immediately asked if we'd seen a green Renault en route. Apparently it had been expected in Reggane nine days earlier, and a relative of the missing party was now so frantic that he was on the verge of hiring a car or even a plane to look for the lost group himself. Only at his insistence were the phlegmatic Algerian authorities making a belated effort to track down the Renault: they'd long since given up initiating searches for lost travellers – if indeed they ever undertook them in the first place. Nonetheless, bleak though the Tanezrouft is, it was hard to imagine anyone getting lost in the fine conditions we'd experienced for the last couple of days; clearly a car that was overdue from Bordj by several days had either slipped through Reggane without checking in or was never going to turn up.

Reggane is the southernmost of a string of oases known as the Tuat which feed on the subterranean Saoura river that is itself reliably replenished from the Atlas' southern run-off. Palmeries and small cultivable patches prosper here due to an intricate system of drainage tunnels and shafts called *foggaras*, a system that originated in ancient Persia and was probably introduced to the region by the Jews who fled there from Cyrenaica in the second century AD. However this all makes the Tuat sound more interesting than it actually is and as far as I was concerned our off-road adventure was now over and it only remained to drive home.

We rode with the Hanomag north to Adrar, Mike winning the war by giving Ingrid a ride there on the back of his bike. As we joined up for a parting lunch in a deserted hotel, I was struck down with the "Green Rivers", the debilitating intestinal blight which had already smitten Clive. Camped by the roadside on the way to Timimoun that evening, I reposed wretchedly with my sleeping bag unzipped, ready to repeat the periodic stagger over a mound to purge my innards.

We finally outran the Hanomagsters next day with me flopped in the back of the van like a wet sheet and Mark at the wheel, and a day later headed up to El Golea, passing low outliers of the Grand Erg Occidental – a vast sea of sand dunes into which the whole of Great Britain would fit with room to spare. Mike rode up alongside the cab asking for his camera to photograph the rather ordinary dunes.

'Further on,' I mouthed, pointing ahead, 'there's some better dunes further on.'

Mike stubbornly insisted on being passed his equipment while I tried to impress on him via Mark that 'There are some BETTER LOOKING DUNES further on!' Which indeed there were – I stopped there in wonder every time I passed the well known spot. Furious at my intransigence, Mike thumped the side of the van with his fist and yelling the now customary expletives, tore off ahead.

Presently we alighted among my superior sands for a break. Livid with everyone, especially me, Mike grabbed his camera gear, slung it over his shoulder and tried riding up onto the dune, getting bogged down almost immediately on the steep slope. To add to his fury his stalled bike wouldn't start. We looked on, letting his tantrum run its course. By now I felt that the roles had reversed and that the volatile Mike, alternately hilariously self-mocking, co-operative, facetious and enraged, had assumed the mantle of group pariah.

The four remaining *SMeTards* droned northwards to the sea without incident and after a few days' delay at the docks sailed back to Marseille where Mark and Mike Motorailed home. Clive and I took our time and went visiting, getting stranded, penniless, near a mountain village when the 101 again caught an overnight chill. After that we drove the thing non-stop to Calais and home.

Though the tour had been a valuable experience and had extended my knowledge of the Sahara and Ford York engines, I accepted without surprise that I was not cut out to be a tour operator and leader of men. I felt uncomfortable with the disparity of experience, and the burden of responsibility was hardly liberating. And I liked being by myself (or at least a stranger) too much. It would have been interesting to explore the others' view of their experience but we either drifted apart or the subject became inevitably fossilised into "remember when..." anecdotes.

Just recently I was about to put myself into their position and pay £3000 to join a German-organised *twenty*-bike expedition to southern Libya, Chad and the far northern Ténéré.* Initially I was thrilled by the idea of paying someone else to undertake all the complexities of mounting such an ambitious venture and there was certainly no other way of getting to Chad's Tibesti mountains, short of a full-on expedition. But even before I sent away my deposit I was planning to split from the huge party once the remote bits had been explored and head home across the Ténéré and via Mauritania. Twenty German bikers would certainly have conjured up some interesting group dynamics and I was intrigued to see how something ten times more risky than SMT would have got on. It might have made good viewing, but I knew that only once I sneaked off would my real adventures begin.

---

* If fact it was the German trip which was to have been the subject of this book but, pitiless publisher's advance already paid, the tour got abridged and I dropped out, having to resort to my own torpid desert memoirs to fill these pages. Bad luck!

INTO WEST AFRICA

I'm going where the sun keeps shining
through the pouring rain
Going where the weather suits my clothes
Banking off on the northeast winds
Sailing on summer breeze
An' skipping over the ocean like a storm.

Everybody's Talkin'
(theme from Midnight Cowboy)

'Bab in the Cab

I'd pictured this idealised situation back home: sitting on my bag under a tree at some heat-caked Sahelian crossroads, waiting idly for a lift. Something would eventually turn up: this wasn't the Sahara after all. Sat a mile or two east of Richard Toll in northern Senegal, the rank streets of Banjul and Dakar were thankfully behind me now, which left only one more West African city, Bamako, to research for the guidebook I was updating

A 504 lumbered slowly and noisily up the hill, trailing a veil of oily fumes. Hunching forward to stand up, I recognised the usual press of bodies against the windows and I rolled right back against the tree trunk. Red and green ants busied themselves around my feet as I mulled over the practicalities of spending the night around here if need be. I'd inevitably have to spend a few nights *en brousse* (in the bush) to stretch the paltry fee for this assignment.

The plan was to taxi-hop my way in a drooping eastward curve along the Senegal River down to Kidira, a rail stop on the Dakar-Bamako line. There I'd intercept the twice-weekly train to Mali's capital where I'd paused briefly a few years before, having finally ridden across the desert. On that occasion I'd sped nervously through the sub-Saharan states, but on this back-country excursion I was looking forward to a slow-paced reprieve between the swarming West African metropolises.

An old man on a moped wearing the cap of a *marabout* holy man, robe tucked between his legs, buzzed out of Richard Toll heading east. Behind him an old Berliet truck gathered itself up for a run at the hill and passed him much too close. Alarmed, he veered off onto the roadside gravel, extending his feet ready for a crash, but got back on course and passed me without a glance.

This must be what all those backpackers do, I thought. Take off across Africa with a duffel bag and a wodge of cash. There was even a book called *Backpacking in Africa*. I'd never read it but wondered what on earth the guide could say. It was like those *Cycling in Europe* books I used to sell in a bookshop. What could such a book tell you that you couldn't work out with a map and a bit of imagination? Guidebooks I'd decided were inspirational aids which people bought during their Monday lunch break after reading a fabulous article in the weekend's colour supplements.

Bush taxi-ing my way in a clockwise arc across the north of Senegal was my way of making this country interesting. On a scale of ease of travel in West Africa, Senegal comes close to the top; on the fascination scale it comes in safe and low. As far as I was concerned it was too flat, too Frenchified and too developed to offer an adventurous tourist much immediate gratification.

There was even a Club Med down south in the tropical Casamance region. Reputedly the only one in sub-Saharan Africa, I'd always imagined a Club Med to be an adult Butlins resplendent with all the sophistication the fish-'n-chips Brits couldn't muster. Visiting the Casamance a few weeks later, a mellow de-Islamicised region of mango trees, tidal lagoons and a network of inexpensive rural *campements*, I found it indeed a lovely place for a holiday, enjoying a lull in the revenue-ruining insurgence of the MFDC (*Mouvement des Forces Démocratiques de la Casamance*) separatist front. Other than the tropical Casamance and the acquired appeal of Dakar, Senegal comprised a riverless, sun-baked interior of Sahelian villages, a neo-Casamançaise beach enclave south of Dakar, and the meagre wildlife of the Nikolo-Koba National Park in the southeast.

In fact there were few tangible sights to make for anywhere in West Africa. Hardly any relics from the prosperous medieval empires of Ghana, Mali* and Songhai remained, and Africa certainly wasn't the $10/day destination many presumed. As a round-the-worlding American I later met in Bamako pointed out, "It's expensive and what's there to see? Give me Asia any day." As if to bear out his negative view, he got brutally mugged that evening – his first such experience in months of world travel.

So a bush taxi ride beneath the Mauritanian frontier to Kidira was a way of getting to the heart of the West African experience. I didn't miss having a motorbike one bit. It was a relief to be away from the tiresome preoccupations of fuel, nagging engine noises, documentation and endless lesser paranoias that cast a cloud of anxiety between yourself and your surroundings. Independent mobility may be indispensable in the desert, but West Africa was far too stimulating to be wasted on yet more motorbiking.

In refreshing contrast to the uptight Arab north, West Africa seemed to me a vibrant and friendly place, bursting with an irrepressibly chaotic *joie de vivre* that I'd not encountered anywhere else. With a far less rigourous interpretation of the Islamic creed the West African way of life felt exuberantly sensual – as exemplified by its wonderful music – and for me made a perfect counterpoint to the solitary drama of the desert. This vivid change from the dour Maghreb to the jovial gregarity of Niger or Mali was a wonder. The vivacious women and mischievous children which

* Neither of these appellations refer to the present day countries of the same name.

you'd thought had disappeared for good, the pernicious intoxicants of beer and ganja, dazzling toothsome grins instead of malign sneers. But, though one might learn to deal with the teeming taxi parks and markets, this vitality would eventually drive an individualistic, retiring and satiable European round the bend. But not yet.

A white minibus came uphill and I raised my arm lazily, finger pointing to the ground, and was a little surprised when it slowed down. Grabbing my bag I walked up to the "conductor" and enquired:

'*Podor*?'

'*Oui*, get in.'

From the look of it, this was one of the newest bush taxis on the continent; in neighbouring Mali or Guinea such a pristine vehicle would have been used exclusively for presidential family picnics. I was irritated when, as on that morning's ride from St Louis, someone gave up the desirable front seat for me. I detested this preference but had long since resigned myself to never simply being treated as a normal passenger. The only time a *toubab* (white foreigner) like myself might lose the roomy front seat was when an attractive woman came on board. Having a '*bab* in your cab might lend you some cred, but far better to have a good looking woman by your side.

The bush taxi union must have a fair amount of clout in West Africa. While every single seat is expected to carry as many passengers as possible, there's still a strictly classified trio of crew. At the top of the pyramid is the aloof *pilot* who commands the steering wheel and with it the fate of the bus. At his most animated you might see him drop his veil and spit, or relay an irate complaint to a passenger obstructing his vision.

Conductors are as garrulous and bossy as their drivers are taciturn and disdainful, ordering the already cramped passengers to budge up still further at every stop. "There's no room," they complain, "let him sit with them, they're thin!" Then an argument erupts, the loud voices and accusing fingers attracting passers-by to enjoy the show or contribute to the commotion. In fact a new verb is needed here: to commote; to get involved in some kind of altercation; to not mind your own business because you have an opinion to express. Out here, people aren't shy of getting involved in passing disputes and two peripheral commoters might lock horns over their own quarrel while the main event rumbles to its own conclusion. In such unreserved societies, social interaction thrives on a mild but unresentful belligerence; it's a way of saying "I'm alive, I exist, I have something to say."

Last in line comes the scrag end thirteen year-old apprentice, the baggage handler who lashes your broken bicycle, squawking chickens or sackful of melons to the roof rack. As the *taxi brousse* – anything from a Sixties' Peugeot to a new Japanese minibus – fills up, conductor and handler cling nonchalantly to any exterior handhold. Stuffed inside the unventilated bus, we sardines envy their breeze.

As the minibus sped up onto the inland plateau the temperature rose with it. From time to time I glimpsed the Senegal River to our left and, unable to write, tried to memorise details so as to add a molecule of authenticity to my eventual account. One day a reader might exclaim, "Look, there's the river just like it says. So someone *did* come this way after all!" We stopped at Dagana where a small boy handed the conductor a bundle; someone got out and walked off into the bush and, at the far end of town two women got in. No one paid me the slightest bit of attention. After Banjul and Dakar, it felt wonderful to be so eminently invisible.

The road veered away from the river, the trees thinned and the grass turned to patches of scraggy straw. Within an hour we reached the turn off for Podor, the ancient centre of gold trading from which its name *Port d'or* reputedly derives. As usual there was a small amount of confusion, I'd paid to Podor but the minibus was heading straight on. Things were sorted out when a driver waiting in a decrepit 504 was slipped the fee and I and a few Podorians squeezed into his wreck. With a couple of push starts the taxi staggered into life, weaving its way to town, flat out in second gear.

In the deserted town square there was no sign of the hotel I was supposed to check out, but a bench beneath a huge silk cotton tree offered a good spot for a siesta. All the time the expectation that my presence was about to cause some commotion nagged me, but for the moment I lay back and let the late-afternoon heat draw me out.

Relentless scrutiny is the bane of travelling in Africa. In Dakar I had to literally steel myself before setting foot outside my hotel, whereafter I'd march about with a "don't fuck with me" glare pasted across my face. Too many want to be your friend – and by no means are all insincere. Distinguishing the hustlers from the helpful wasn't always easy and the whole game was ultimately unwinnable. Taxi drivers kept stopping to give me a lift because Dakar is like LA: clued-up whites don't walk the streets unless they're poor or mad or looking for a taxi.

The friendly patter of stones and bashful whispers of "*M'sier...m'sieur*" brought me out of my doze as the sun sank low over the square. Refreshed and hungry, I got up to search Podor's few sandy streets for the promised accommodation. It was not an especially interesting or attractive town, a grid of uniform mud brick walls and dusty riverbank trees most notable as being the home of the musician Baaba Maal. In less than twenty minutes I was back at the *gare*, having found not so much as a kiosk open.

By a hut in the corner a woman sat spread legged around an oil drum converted into a wood-burning stove. No, there was no hotel in town she told me, but I could stay in one of the concrete shacks and take the morning taxi back to the highway. She gave me some dinner too: a hunk of meat hung behind her and, shooing away the flies, she carved off some slithers of meat and threw them into a pan with as much onion. A litre mug of water was placed in front of me and someone was sent to tidy up my cell.

Darkness had fallen and there was nothing left to do but surrender myself to one of the most uncomfortable nights of my life. The sedentary Africans have a fear of sleeping out in the bush, an understandable collective memory from former times when wild game was a real threat. Only the reviled nomads sleep out under the stars;: *toubabs* surely demand the privacy of their own room. Inside the windowless storeroom only a thin mattress separated me from the concrete floor and I was urged to close my door. Within minutes the stifling accumulation of the day's heat became utterly unbearable and for the next few hours I lay there wide awake in the dark, sweating and tossing and migrating between cool bits of sheet.

Then the real battle began. Unidentifiable creatures energised by the night started dive-bombing me with repulsive, heavy thuds. As I sprang up in terror at the thought of death by virulent cockroach, the pests fluttered off. A minute or two would pass and they'd attack again. And again. By midnight I could stand them and the heat no longer and, though loathe to cause my hostess offence, I crawled out into the car park to let the beasts of the bush tear me apart.

Outside it was the mosquitoes who held sway. On this trip I was experimenting without the malaria prophylatics which travellers to the tropics are advised to take. Suspecting that the whole travellers' health business was just a huge drug company conspiracy dependant on a multi-million pound "Better safe than sorry" attitude, tonight was the night I might end up sorry.

Though only some mosquitoes carry malaria, the best way to avoid the disease is to not get bitten in the first place, so I wrapped my head in my Mozz-Off-soaked *cheche* and spent the rest of the night slapping my thighs and

ankles, shins and knees, fuming against the irascible whine
of the world's deadliest creatures. A few weeks later in the
Casamance I had a bizarre Livingstone-and-Stanley
encounter with an old Africa hand who was engaged in a
similar job for a rival guide book series. When I told him
and his doctor wife that I was skipping anti-malaria pills
they looked at me as if I'd just admitted to copulating with
a gonorrhoeic baboon.

Dawn mercifully arrived and with it a reason to get up
off the dirt and slump dazed and itching against a wall. At
the oil drum, breakfast was being served: black coffee and
bread.

"*Bien dormi?*" the woman enquired.

"*Ah oui, pas mal,*" I lied, wincing at the bitter brew.

'*Rosogui?*' the conductor of a blue and yellow Saviem *car
rapide* asked me.

'*Oui*' I affirmed hurriedly, not knowing what they meant,
but accepting the van was at least going in the right direction. I was herded into the back where three benches
accommodated the passengers in bovine-class comfort and
where no one talked, creating the self-conscious, eye-avert-
ing isolation of a London tube. Neither did anyone eat and
only rarely drank; all were resigned to stoically enduring
the noise, heat, and bumps of the long journey.

'*Ros'gui, Bakel*' the two conductors yelled as the car
pulled into a village. I watched their back bumper antics
with amusement, rap-rap-rapping on the tailgate as another fare sat themselves down, then casually allowing the van
to move off before climbing on with a lazy skip and a jump.
At one point an attractive Moorish girl in an orange outfit
was helped aboard. The more playful of the two conductors
spotted me appraising her and gave me a tug down of his
lower eyelid and a knowing "fancy her do you?" nod. He
tapped her shoulder and pointed me out with some muttered comment and she looked away, grinning shyly. It was
the highlight of my day.

By late afternoon we'd reached the town of Ouro Sogui, not my intended destination according to my map but clearly the major regional centre and transport hub. The Saviem pushed and nudged down the crowded main drag lined with colourful stalls selling cassettes, cigarettes, plastic goods, cosmetics and other domestic knick-knackery

Spotting the *Auberge Sogui* as we'd passed, I found my way back there and, with the fan cranked up to lift-off speed, flopped out on the hot bed. Pinned down by lethargy, the need to undertake my research plod nagged at me until my professional curiosity recovered and I set off around the now empty streets. I found nothing new bar a couple of cafés and, satisfied that duty had been done, returned to the hotel. A dusty *harmattan* (a hot and dry wind from the northeast), which had mired the day's scrawny Sahelian vistas, began blowing hard across the hotel's open terrace as I shared an oversized melon with the fatalist proprietor. Down on the street all was deserted, the frenetic daytime activity having fizzled away. Nothing stirred except dust and rubbish borne along by the wind.

Arriving at the *gare* bright and early next day I found the same *car* and crew doing the next stage on to Bakel.

'*Tu vas à Bakel aujourd'hui?*' asked one of the conductors who recognised me.

'*Oui.*'

'*C'est dur. La route est mauvaise, très poussièreuse.*'

Sure enough, a short distance out of town the Saviem came to the end of the sealed road and began thumping, swerving and crashing along the potholed dirt track to Semmé. The faces of the conductors became coated with the pale dust beaten up off the ruined track. Around us the drab plains was beginning to rise into low hills from which dry creek beds cut down to the Senegal river. With the emerging relief, the scraggy straw of the plains became thick grass speckled with sturdy trees.

By the time we got to Bakel, my next staging post, I'd

developed an affection for the softly undulating country-side, while the town itself, older and denser than Ouro Sogui's bland new town expanse, restored my under stimulated mood still further. The van rolled to a halt by the market and as I eased myself out, crook-backed and numb-bummed, the conductor pointed the way to the town's only hotel and shook my hand at having endured the two-day run from Podor.

Bakel was the only point of interest on my north Senegalese voyage of discovery. Tucked like a secret between the hills and the river, its old core looked much as it might have done a hundred and fifty years earlier, when René Caillié lived here as a governor following his return from Timbuktu, the first European to do so

The *Hôtel d'Islam* seemed to date from that era: a ring of balconies serving tiny cells around a courtyard and a flat roof where a cooler night's rest could be enjoyed. As before, my room had cooked up a suffocating heat over the day. Opening the shutters and stirring the wobbly fan into action, I again collapsed on the bed, exhausted by nothing more than sitting all day in the back of a van. My limbs drooped over the sides of the ancient bed as I listened to the noises of the street; barking dogs, the spluttering protests of a shagged-out moped, the crowing of cocks and the muttering of passers-by.

Within an hour I regained enough energy to see just how bad the shower looked. Refreshed and revived, I went out to assess the town, though as in Ouro Sogui, things for the visitor "to see and do" were sparse. I ambled down to the river bank to have a look at the far Mauritanian shore. It looked much like Senegal, but I knew the Islamic republic to be a singular country, an Arabic land but with the moderating influence of black West Africa.

I crouched on a promontory and looked downriver. The dust settling on the orange twilit scene gave it a fuzzy Turneresque quality. The old fort looked down onto the narrow meandering river where a couple of *pirogues* (dugout canoes) were engaged in some arcane task, maybe even smuggling. Everything took on a pinky-fawn hue as the land gave up its blanket of heat – that brief undisturbed interlude when the flies returned to their lairs and the mosquitoes stretched their wings and sharpened their probes. There was little more a tourist guidebook needed to know about Bakel.

Back on the main street, a coloured-bulbed take-away served me a couple of *shawarmas*, the Lebanese kebabs which are West Africa's urban fast-food staple. With them came a litre of crimson *bissap*, a refreshing Ribena-like drink made from hibiscus juice. I'd seen the luridly coloured drink sold in knotted plastic bags at truck stops on the way here, but had been too timid to buy some until someone did so for me. As I sucked the bottle dry I wondered what a hibiscus flower looked like, where they grew and how many it took to get a litre of juice like this.

Walking back to the hotel the long way a Land Rover loaded with French tourists stopped to ask me the way to a hotel. I directed them to the *Islam* but they'd already been there, exclaiming,

'*Pah, c'est un vrai trou!*' (a dump)

'*Ah, c'est tout je pense.*'

'*Bien, merci.*' And off they went, tipping along the washed out track like a boat in a swell. I returned to my room and slumped beneath the rattle and hum of the fan.

The grumpy *patron* didn't take kindly to my request for breakfast next morning, there not being enough guests to bother filling the kettle. As I turned to leave, I saw a gorgeous woman looking at me.

'*Ca va*? she asked with a suggestive smile.

'*Oui, bonjour,*' I responded, taking the chance to ask her where the post office might be. She stepped outside and pointed out the way to the square.

'*En face du fort,*' she said, flicking one hand up the street while the other rested on her canted hip, and flashing me another smile that no amount of Beverly Hills dental engineering could hope to replicate. At the post office another charming woman pointed out that though she may be at work she was actually *en grève*, something I eventually understood to mean on strike. A low-grade flirting crackled across the counter of a type I'd never expect in my local branch and these twin episodes got me thinking about the uncanny enchantment of some Senegalese women.

Their beauty wasn't just a combination of face and figure, it stemmed from their extraordinary grace, poise and not least from the clothes they wore to such striking effect. Even when they weren't carrying a calabash on their heads they walked with a velvety, straight-necked saunter. They looked great and they knew it.

I perceived a distinction in morale between the sexes. Though it may be assumed that Senegalese men have more opportunity for self-fulfilment, I had a fleeting, if unfashionably reactionary notion that men tended to waste their freedom chasing western models of self-improvement while the women just got on with it. They seemed to know who and what they were and accepted this, indifferent to change. This focus shone out with a sisterly certainty in their daily lives. Wrecked men were a common sight, begging, resentful or lost, while the women acted vital and alive.

On the highway next morning an ageing minibus took us all for the hour's run to Kidira, a memorably picturesque track wending through the hills and trees and creeks. At Kidira we were dropped outside the police station were everyone "booked in" and dispersed. I followed the rails down to the river and as I washed and my clothes with the other menfolk from town, I glanced upstream where eight years earlier I'd ridden my double-punctured bike through the shallow river which divided Senegal from Mali. There was a new all-season road bridge spanning the Falemé river now, and as my clothes dried on a rock and a couple of boys did their best to playfully drown their mate, I thought back to Helmut and the first time I'd managed to cross over the Sahara into West Africa.

Inshallah; Bukrah; Mahlesh

(God willing; Later; What does it matter)
Arabic sayings

Set in by a bend in the huge Arak gorge, halfway between In Salah and Tam, there's a roadhouse that has, over the years, evolved into something of a personal milestone. Stopping here on my first ever Saharan trip, I'd felt rather pleased with myself, a dusty desert dilettante of three days heading south into the unknown. A bowl of lumpen cous cous in the rudimentary café made a hearty and overdue snack. Service didn't come with a smile, but I was becoming accustomed to the stern Algerian psyche.

One excessively hot September a few years later I was obliged to spend a little longer than I wanted in Arak. Having thoughtlessly ridden my bike onto an unset section of tarmac just north of the roadhouse – ruining the painstaking road repairs in the process – I was placed under immediate "hut arrest" by the furious army commander. Luckily he only kept my passport for two or three days, but even this short delay put my ephemeral goal on that deranged two-week trip beyond reach. You can plan all you like in the Sahara and prepare yourself for anything, but things rarely if ever turn out as you expect.

So now, third time round, I'd decided to adopt a "go with the flow" philosophy, a fatalistic optimism which was to free me of the xenophobic agonies which had embittered the end of my first trip. This time I'd just go south, cross the Sahara, and head for the Ivory Coast or Dakar, who knows? If I didn't make it over the desert for whatever reason then so be it. I had a lightly loaded bike, some experience and a Good Attitude. All were to serve me well although the trip was not, of course, without its dramas.

Sitting against Arak's shady café wall breaking my teeth on a half-day-old baguette I heard another lone biker ride up to the fuel pumps. German, slightly eccentric and scruffy, wearing John Lennon shades and sitting on a sheepskin saddle: not the usual Paris–Dakar racer clone. His appearance combined with his ridiculously overloaded bike suggested a First Timer, a Young Romantic setting off to explore the African highways in search of adventure and authenticity. All this divined in a few seconds at 30 metres! He rode up to where I was sitting and peeled off his specs and open-face helmet – the latter signifying his reluctance to hide behind the enigmatic machismo of a full face "lid".

'*Bonjour*,' I said.

'Hi, English, ya?'

'Ah ha.' (Damn, suddenly talking English abroad was like waking up from a particularly good dream!)

I was looking for someone with whom to ride the piste to the south side of the Sahara and out here social preliminaries are compressed: what needs to be said or done, is said or done. Helmut was also heading south and although his bike was untypical of the average German desert biker, or perhaps because of it, we decided to meet up again in Tam and cross the desert together.

North of Arak the Highway landscape is flat, barren and bleak, save for some alluring dune ranges. But things get a bit more interesting south of the gorge, with denuded gran-

ite domes unpeeling – or to be precise, exfoliating huge lay-
ers of rock like drying onion skin. Distant mountain clus-
ters, some rounded like mosques, others pointed like
Matterhorns, add intrigue to the varied landscape.

As these mountains subside the Highway, or what there
is of it, passes the small mausoleum of Moulay Hassan, the
tomb of a holy man who died here on his way to Mecca.
According to Saharan superstition, all passers-by are
expected to pay their respects by circling the white tomb
three times before continuing on their way south. A short
distance beyond the tomb the burned-out wreck of a VW
combi stands as a monument to those who ignore the custom. The fact that I have never done the rounds may
explain a lot about my Saharan experiences...

Emerging onto a sandy plain, the piste onto which I'd
been detoured since Arak crossed the closed-off Highway,
but a stone barricade seemingly pushed aside tempted me
to ride for a few vacuous miles along the smooth tarmac.
Within an hour I was on the sharp end of a depressingly
familiar tirade.

'*T'as roule combien de kilometres sur la route ferme?*'
demanded an apoplectic soldier who'd already gathered a
band of similar transgressors behind him, most of them
French students doing Tam on the cheap in farmers' hatch-
backs.

'Er, *quinze*,' I lied.

'*Bon, tu restes ici quinze jours!*' he snapped. '*Papiers!*'

I dutifully surrendered my passport, enquiring whether
there was any water here.

'*Non!*' he snapped.

This prognosis was not good. Before half my sentence
had passed I would be dead of thirst along with the others.
To be fair on myself, this wasn't a new road waiting to set
like last time, but a perfectly usable stretch of blacktop –
something of a lucky break for drivers of low-powered
2CVs and the like. I expected to be fined or detained for a
couple of days at the most, but before I'd even looked

around for a place to camp, my documents were returned and I was dismissed. Paying off the guides who led me back to the approved track, I wondered whether the inviting open barricade/closed road was a scam to fleece the foreign traffic.

By sundown the next day I was installed in the campsite at the southern end of Tamanrasset – along with just about all the other overlanders who were in the area for Christmas. It was a busy time in the desert, boom-time for Saharan motor tourism, not least because the Algerian dinars that were easily obtained on the black market effectively reduced fuel prices to pre-Oil Crisis levels.

Furthermore the prestigious Paris–Dakar Rally, established a few years earlier, now had French TV viewers transfixed by the daily dramas which were screened at peak viewing times. Concern at the extravagant spectacle's dubious taste was only slowly beginning to be addressed; most years at least one African villager was run down as million-pound double-engined racing trucks tore through their settlement, though most deaths were limited to competitors. Oddly enough these fatalities, which added greatly to the event's gladiatorial glamour, were not among bikers, but truckers: support vehicles which were also engaged in the race. When they overturned at full speed no roll bar on earth could stop the twenty-ton juggernaut from crushing its occupants.

The year Helmut and I set off across the Sahara, the Rally's organiser, Thierry Sabine, had founded an appeasing and cleverly-named "Paris du Coeur" project. A certain portion of the contestants' huge entry fees was to be invested in new well pumps for the desiccated Sahel. Die-hard detractors rightly pointed out that more wells in a drought stricken region was the worse kind of short term solution. Such a project would encourage re-migration to the new wells, thereby lowering the subterranean water table still further and making matters worse.

Himself an ex-competitor who had nearly perished in an earlier rally, Sabine had made the course harder than ever that year. Near impossible thousand-kilometre days ensured that only the very fittest, mollycoddled and amphetamine-fuelled competitors on the best machinery could hope to keep up. The "Dakar" was fast loosing its once admired amateur flavour, becoming nothing more than a barely finishable circus for the likes of Citröen, Porsche or Yamaha to demonstrate their Rally-winning prototypes.

Sabine lost his life that year, crashing his trademark helicopter in a sandstorm near Timbuktu while gallantly looking for stragglers. His ashes were scattered in the northern Ténéré and it's a mark of the impact he had on his countrymen that Michelin named the spot "Arbre Thierry Sabine" on their "953" map. Without his charismatic leadership the Rally lost its way for a few years. Algeria became too dangerous and bandits in Libya harassed or killed competitors. An alternative Paris–Cape Town version was a flop, its tedious images of red earth tracks cutting through impenetrable jungles lacking the stunning desert vistas which so fascinated the viewers back home.

These days the Dakar doesn't even start in France and is a relatively emasculated fortnight's affair bereft of its former cubic dollar factory support. Re-profiled back towards the amateur racer with £10,000–15,000 to spend, it now runs in a loop from Dakar through the Mauritanian and Malian deserts to the jungles of Guinea before ending with the usual razzmatazz on the beaches near Dakar.

Helmut arrived in Tamanrasset a day later, an exhaust pipe strapped to the back of his seat proof that already the piste had scored a point. Before heading south we decided to do a trial run up to the pass at Assekrem, sixty miles from town in the heart of the Hoggar mountains; "a sight not to be missed" according to the Sahara Handbook. It would also be a good chance to get the measure of each other and our bikes before attempting the desert crossing.

Packing enough gear for an overnight stop, we probed around the eastern edges of Tam, searching for the piste which led to the mountains. Soon we passed Jojo's Spring, a natural source of water that, unlike Tam's scarce supply, remained unrationed. To our north the distinctive volcanic plug of Iharen offered a hint of the spectacle ahead. Presently the piste rose up onto the sombre volcanic plateau of the Atakor, the Hoggar's dramatic core where, even on bikes, we struggled to find a hand's width of track that hadn't become corrugated.

Within a couple of hours we reached the turn-off which led up to the pass of Assekrem: a narrow set of hairpins gouged by the spinning tyres of cars scrabbling for traction. And then the track flattened out and we were astride the 9000'-high saddle where a stone hut housed overnighters come to view the dawn.

The aptly named hermitage of Père Charles Foucauld, perched another couple of hundred feet up a steep path, was the reason we all came here. It was only from that point that the renowned views across to the fluted volcanic plugs could be appreciated. And as we all knew, this homage was best paid at dawn when the low sun added a preternatural drama to the whole show: more effort than I was prepared to make.

The contrary Helmut, who was endeavouring to be a humble traveller and not a simpering tourist, turned down the opportunity to see for himself, settling for a half-ascent on which his iconoclastic principles would not be compromised. I appreciated his point of view, but was genuinely curious to experience this Saharan "must see" even if it wasn't at dawn. I panted on up the track, the days of idle motorbiking and altitude taking their toll as I passed fulfiled returnees scampering back down to their jeeps. Once up at the top I was astonished to find that I had the summit to myself.

Assekrem is to the Sahara what the Monument Valley is

to the US and in his book *Sailing to Timbuctoo* John Marriner (an over-curious commentator who even chased conscripts into brothels to "see what on earth was happening") found himself deeply moved on reaching the hermitage situated atop what he described as "a frenzy of torn lava".

> I never felt more alone and yet so close to something in all my life. It was like being at sea in a great gale at night, with one's emotions tumbling about one in huge waves, each one threatening destruction, yet relenting just in time for the inevitable next wave to begin. Wave after wave poured over me. I was drowning now. I could hear the sound of fury and then a great peace, like you get, they say, just after you die, or when you are hanged by the neck until you are dead, or when someone in a dim underground passage, where you have been told to walk after sentence of death has been passed, takes aim and you hear nothing but you are shot in the back of your neck. I am not a deeply religious man – more interested, I admit in the esoteric than in the spiritual values of religion. I only know that when I found myself again I was on my knees and the tears were running quietly down my cheeks.

My reaction wasn't quite so strong but an indubitable and unexpected spiritual frisson did bring a lump to my throat as I entered the tiny chapel built by the priest.

Foucauld's story is a regular staple of Saharan travelogues and I can barely bring myself to go through it all again. Suffice to say the Vicomte Charles de Foucauld came from an aristocratic background, was orphaned at five and later graduated from St Cyr (France's prestigious officer's academy), after which he became a notorious *bon viveur* while stationed in North Africa.

Sent home in disgrace after attempting to install a mistress close to his barracks, he mysteriously outgrew his fecklessness and decided to attempt something worthwhile with his life. After a period spent wandering around the then hostile Morocco disguised as a merchant Jew, he turned to the cloth and took up a life of uncompromising asceticism. Turning to Algeria, Foucauld's piety won respect from even the most hardened agnostics and he was eventually persuaded to relocate to Tamanrasset, where the Tuareg were considered ripe for conversion. Proselytising little, he further earned the admiration of the Ahaggar through his selfless concern for their well-being. The political machinations of the First World War powers led to his clumsy assassination by a rogue band of Tuareg in 1916.

Contrary to popular belief Foucauld didn't actually live up here, but spent most of his time in Tamanrasset and only endured a couple of spells at Assekrem. His library stands alongside the simple chapel and tiny room in which he slept on bare slabs, and in it you can inspect his painstaking transcriptions of the Tuareg *tifinar* script. A visitors' book records the names of pilgrims from all over the world:

"Top place – totally unreal!!!" Kim from Bungee, New South Wales.

"Our spirits soar in the presence of God and this holy man." A couple from New England.

"The African Express rises at dawn and takes no prisoners. This place nearly beats the Ruwenzori." Jonny and Giles from Hampshire.

"Dieu est ici." Sabina from Cologne.

I felt privileged to have the place to myself. A freak lull in the waves of visitors coursing up and down the mountainside had transformed my experience into a poignant memory, not just a dutiful shuffle spent ducking telephoto crossfire. To the south the vestiges of old volcanoes looked like they'd erupted from the earth's core only yesterday. Beds of age-old scree lay piled against the fluted prongs of rock. Elsewhere on the mini plateau, a weather station recorded the severe climatic variations, just as it had done in Foucauld's day. The refractory Helmut may have had a point giving this Saharan Taj Mahal a miss, but that reputation was based on something special, and I'd been lucky enough to catch it. I rejoined him back at the pass as the sun was setting on what was to be a cold night.

'Was it good?' he asked without mockery.

'It was actually. Pretty amazing. There was no one there.'

Bad Day at Laouni

With twilight falling Helmut and I rode down the far side of the pass, a rougher, less frequented piste which also eventually led back to Tam. Finding a patch of flat ground a short distance from the col we made camp, scraping together a few twigs for a meagre fire. It was a barren, cheerless place and as soon as we had fed ourselves, we curled up into our sleeping bags and dozed off.

Next morning, stiff from our exposed bivouac, we continued our careful descent from the hills, Helmut having to walk his heavy ex-police bike down the steeper rock steps. Later, as the piste flattened out to follow sandy oueds, the hapless Helmut lost control of his cumbersome machine and the BMW came to rest in perfect balance – upside down. I turned the undamaged machine back on its wheels while he looked on bemused, not quite sure what had happened.

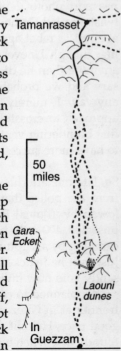

The ground spread out into the Atakor's foothills, our pace speeded up and we momentarily lost sight of each other – an easy mistake to make when riding with an unfamiliar partner. Helmut had gone one way round a hill and I another. Not seeing each other, I'd gone back thinking he'd fallen off, while he'd rushed ahead in an attempt to catch me up. Suddenly fear struck home as I sat there all alone on an unknown track. Climbing up a rise to give me a better view, I turned off my bike to help detect Helmut's rorty engine note and sure enough there he was, riding back towards me. We'd learnt our lesson and stuck close together all the way back to Tam.

Christmas Day came and went like any other and Helmut, who'd found the mountain tracks hard going, made some small repairs and lightened his load for the long ride south. In the afternoons we'd play at being humble nomads, boiling up mint tea in his little enamelled teapot and talking a little of our lives back in Europe. The subdued Helmut had a shadow of inhibition about him, a manifestation of his scorn of conventionality and his reluctance to belong. In this respect he felt like something of a kindred spirit. His passport photo depicted an unrecognisable portrait of a twisty curled Orthodox Jew. Perhaps this journey was his attempt to rebel against a stiflingly conservative upbringing, though I never probed his motives for coming here anymore than he did mine. Such questions were unnecessary and we probably couldn't have explained ourselves anyway. I merely identified with his nonconformist approach to crossing the desert. He reminded me of my first blundering venture into these parts and I wanted him to have more success than I'd found.

So, late one afternoon we checked out and with a caution from the police that return to Tam was not allowed followed by a jovial *Bonne route*, we headed down into the unsealed 400-mile breach in the trans-Saharan Highway, camping by an upturned wreck at the tarred section's end. Just as it had sucked me in four years ago, the implacable sandy void now invited the two of us to cross its wastes.

We planned to cover the 200-odd miles to the Algerian frontier at In Guezzam in one long day and so set off at a good pace, Helmut piloting his lightened BMW with new-found poise when bits of it weren't falling off. At one point we stopped to help push a bogged-down pick-up out of the sand. Two women sat motionless in the front as the driver struggled to dig the car free. I left wondering how desperate their situation needed to get before the women were called to intervene against Allah's Will and do something to help themselves.

I recognised nothing from my first ride down this piste, though I harboured faint hopes of a nostalgic reunion with the green BMW shell where I'd taken the fateful decision to turn back. Instead, we came across a different casualty, this time a biker paying the price for speeding over the piste. One of the Swiss guys we'd met at the campsite had turned several somersaults after jack-knifing in some unexpectedly soft sand. Though both he and his robust BMW appeared undamaged, for some reason the bike would not start. While its owner chewed his lip Helmut waded in confidently, dismantling bits of engine right down to the pistons, and soon the machine came back to life. Bidding the pair good luck, we promised to meet up at In Guezzam later that evening, though with hindsight we should have added the reflexive Muslim tag when speaking of the future: *Inshallah*, "if God wills it".

As it was, we ran into the Swiss riders again later that afternoon, having somehow overtaken them while lost among the Laouni dunes where the mass of tracks converged down towards the frontier. Struggling through the deep sand, we helped a weary Helmut push his mired bike onto firmer sand and again pledged to meet that evening at the frontier.

All this energetic activity and another couple of spills had so exhausted Helmut that we both agreed, just as soon as we were *sure* we were back on the main piste, to call it a day. Once again Helmut fell off in the soft sand, tearing off some baggage which we stashed on my bike. Weaving on over the dunes, following faintly southerly tracks that soon petered out, I came across a promising rise and turned back to see Helmut once more sprawled in the sand with his bike on its side. This time it was more serious, and the worn out rider got up cradling what he thought was a broken shoulder in his other arm. Helmut and his bike had reached the end of their road. Gaunt-faced from shock, the wounded biker stared as his dying machine bled oil and fuel from cracked casings. Even if we could have fixed it, he couldn't have ridden the bike in his state. I removed his baggage and set up our camp while he wound out a sling from a greasy cravat. His lank frame stooped over the bike, willing it to rise up and carry him on across the desert. But in truth we both knew that his first Saharan motorbiking adventure had come to an end – about 100 miles further south than my own, four years earlier.

While I made a meal, I suggested we torch his ruined bike to make it clear that it had been abandoned and there was no one crawling around in the dunes looking for help. Surprisingly, Helmut agreed, this being a fitting send-off for his erstwhile steed. He squatted down, grimacing in silent pain as I poured the gallons of excess fuel over his stricken machine, led out a fuse of petrol and passed him the matches.

Being only a partially reformed adolescent pyromaniac, I could see that a great photo feature was about to erupt before me and I held a camera and spare film ready to record the fireworks. Clenching the box in his mouth, Helmut struck a match with his good hand and dropped it onto the trail of fuel. Fins of blue and yellow flames licked their way towards the drenched bike and then a resounding WHOOMP!!! wrapped the wreck in a blaze that lit the darkened dunescape around us. Within a minute the flames took hold and combustible components bubbled, sagged and cracked, some occasionally exploding in a spatter of sparks and shrapnel.

We watched fascinated, I a drooling paparazzo, wheeling around, snapping from all angles, Helmut (who didn't carry a camera, watch, or any other such accoutrements) crouched low, gazing passively into the flames. Then he started singing, a sturdy scouting anthem that might have been the Death Lament of BMW owners.

As reality sunk in next morning, Helmut breakfasted on more painkillers and we sorted out how much of his stuff we could carry on my bike. The morose German slung a few items onto the smouldering pyre and then broke off the key in the lock of his prized metal box to give the scavengers something to think about.

From the edge of the dunes where Helmut had fallen we could faintly make out the low rise of the Gara Ecker escarpment which acted as a handrail towards the border and with the two of us squeezed onto my bike we wobbled out of the treacherous Laouni dunes and back onto the main piste we'd so nearly reached. After a couple of hours thrashing the overloaded bike we approached the spread of refugee tents which marked the Algerian frontier post of In Guezzam.

The two Swiss bikers were just leaving and we passed on the news to their amazement. A German couple in a VW campervan also sympathised with the cowed Helmut, but in the police cabin, home to the notoriously intransigent Rachid, compassion was rather less forthcoming.

'*Il est interdit d'abandonner une moto dans le desert.*'

'*Mais je suis tombé et…*'

'*C'est interdit,*' insisted the ruthless Rachid, about whom I'd read. '*Il te faut y retourner et la ramener ici.*'

How Helmut would set about finding, let alone transporting the wreck back to In Guezzam was not Rachid's problem.

Sipping Fantas at the expensive hole-in-the-wall café, we pondered our next move. Hiring a pick-up would doubtless cost a fortune and there was no guarantee of finding the bike anyway. Eventually, after a few hours of cigarette swapping, the heartless Rachid relented and came up with a more reasonable demand; Helmut could simply go down to the police station and fill out a notice of abandonment. The whole charade had been a test to ensure that the distraught German biker had not sold his bike on the side.

The Far Side

The Sahara Handbook painted a forbidding picture of the In Guezzam-Assamaka run. Sixteen miles of very sandy No Man's Land between Algeria and Niger, climaxing in a hill of powdery-soft sand known as *feche-feche* which required a good run up to scale. Dry-mouthed with anxiety, I headed into the emptiness, temporarily perturbed by my sudden solitude, now that Helmut awaited a plane back to Tam. I rode raggedly through churned ruts of sand, worried about the *feche-feche* and anxious not to get lost on this short, unmarked stretch. Panic soon subsided though, as I realised that the Handbook had exaggerated the difficulties, at least on a bike, and I found myself following the faint traces of passing cars across a plain of flat sandy gravel.

Pausing for a break on the cultural threshold separating the Arabic northern Sahara from the unknown south, I decided to photograph myself at this waterless watershed, New

Year's Day 1987. Out of the wind came the notion to take an aerial self-portrait by setting the self-timer and throwing the camera high into the air. Not surprisingly, most of the frames captured by the spinning camera were filled with blue sky or blurred sand, but one shot found me, hands outstretched and face contorted in a split-second of catch-the-camera concentration.

Assamaka turned out to consist of nothing more than a portacabin, a tree and a gloomy adobe café. A bereted soldier took my documents and asked to inspect my baggage. Emptying the valuable items I kept in the tank bag, his eyes locked onto my small camera.

'*Ah, ca c'est pour moi?*'

'*Eh?*' I faked confusion.

'*C'est pour moi?*' he repeated, pointing first at the camera and then at himself. This was my first experience of the dreaded bribery which is said to infest all black African frontiers. Experts generally advise moderate placation to aid speedy service, but I certainly wasn't adding my camera to his collection and as my documents were all in order I decided to bluff it out.

'*Non,*' I said, sounding confused, as if he'd somehow got muddled up with what was his and what was mine.

'*T'as pas un cadeau pour moi?*'

'*Kadowe?*'

'*Oui, un petit cadeau.*'

'*Eh?*' I furrowed my brow in consternation. What was a "kadowe".

'*Tu parles Français?*'

'*Er, non, non parlay Fronze.*'

Though doubtless encountering this stale evasive technique several times a day, he gave up with me, conceding I had little to give away and was not worth the bother.

'*Vos papiers seront prêts demain matin.*'

'*Duh?*' I mouthed, skillfully keeping up the imbecilic act as he returned to the cabin.

Next morning I approached the cabin door cautiously, expecting to get barked out. Instead the commander formally invited me in to sit down.

'Nom?'

'Scott.'

'Anglais?'

'Oui.'

'Bobi Sharlton.'

'Um hm, oui.' Football: the international language of low-brow diplomacy. What had the world come to. He thumbed through the passport, deciphering other visa stamps with pallid interest.

'D'accord. Vas y. Bonne route,' he said after stamping the passport. *'Il faut paye l'assurance à Arlit.*

'Oui monsieur, merci beaucoup,' I acknowledged gratefully, as if I'd just been approved for membership of some exclusive club.

To the southwest a line of oil drums led away from the café and again I felt a pang of apprehension. It was only 125 miles to Arlit and the resumption of the sealed Highway, four hours at most, and the route seemed to be marked with balises all the way. People came and went this way daily, yet for me to ride out into the sands felt absurdly reckless. Summoning up my courage I accelerated into the wilderness, hoping speed would quell my nerves and hasten my arrival. As I calmed myself into a slower, steadier cruise, the marker drums suddenly petered out – as so often happens in the Sahara – taking the tracks with them. Presuming this to be quite normal I carried on, following a compass bearing of around 110° that corresponded with Arlit to the east-southeast. Certain that the Air mountains behind the town would soon appear as a guiding landmark, I concentrated on not straying too far northwards; if I overshot Arlit, my next stop would likely be a forced one, stranded in the northern Ténéré with an empty tank. With no signs to guide me I erred south of my bearing, calculating that if

I did miss Arlit, which seemed quite likely, I need only continue east to intercept the sealed highway linking Arlit with
Agadez to the south.

The mild trepidation of being off-piste but not completely lost nagged me for another hour as I made my own
tracks across sandy oueds and rocky platforms. After an
especially bumpy dry creek crossing I got off to look carefully to the south and east for any hint of relief. Blackened
tree stumps burned by passing nomads resembled balises
and drew my gaze like mirages. I took comfort in the fact
that people had passed this way, once. Turning back to the
bike I realised my baggage had come adrift while crossing
the oued and but for my whim to stop and look around I
would have lost it for good. With hands trembling at my
near if hardly fatal miss I lashed the bags crudely back on
the bike, took another bearing and carried on.

A hundred and twenty five miles had already come and
gone on my speedometer and by rights I should already be
sitting feet up in Arlit with a cigar in one hand and a
Martini in the other. Either it was very close or, more likely,
I'd messed up the navigation. Suddenly it dawned on me
that reading a compass while riding a bike would cause
massive magnetic deflection from the steel tank beneath the
hand-held instrument, and so this time I walked far from
the bike and fixed on another point to the east-southeast.

I didn't take my eyes off that blip on the horizon and
almost didn't notice the ground beneath my wheels becoming corrugated. For once I was overjoyed to be riding over
these loathsome ripples, for they signified only one thing:
the recent and regular passing of many vehicles. Discarding
my blip, I now followed the corrugations religiously, relishing the worst of the vibration which verified my reprieve.
Ahead I thought I spotted some man-made construction –
possibly the uranium mine which the new town of Arlit
had been built to serve.

Meanwhile I was getting hotter and hotter. It was certainly warmer here on the south side of the Sahara, but why

was my back feeling so scorched? Reaching behind to check my bags, I yelped with pain. Bike and baggage were shrouded in windblown flames which were, as I tastelessly observed later, "cooking my loaded jerrican into an incendiary device worthy of a department store at Christmas." Expecting an imminent explosion of twisted steel to tear my back open, I jumped away from the bike just as soon as I could skid to a halt, wrenched off the swelling, flame-blackened container and hurled it away with all my force.

Slowing down had animated the flames which now tucked into my canvas bags as the breeze flicked off bits of clothing and peeling seat vinyl. Stamping out the larger flames, I threw sand over the bike and remains of my gear and flopped to the ground, relieved but unsure whether yet again I'd been very lucky or unlucky.

On the bright side I acknowledged that it was indeed the uranium mine visible a few miles to the south and I could now safely assume that I'd crossed the Sahara. Was it normally like this I wondered, or should I have circled three times round Moulay Hassan's tomb up there near Arak?

Arlit was full of colour and life, a wonderful reward for the eventful days I'd just come through. As I sat in a welcoming restaurant waiting patiently for *steak-frites* and Orangina a trinket vendor worked me over, demonstrating the ingenious mechanism of a medieval-looking padlock and flashing a collection of silver Tuareg crosses and leather wallets. Where was my meal, I wondered. Perhaps the chef was in league with the hawker and even now awaiting the "successful sale" thumbs up. Sure enough, as soon as negotiations for three crosses had been wrapped up, the tough meat and wrinkled *frites* arrived. The salesman and a couple of kids watched me eat. They must see us self-satisfied Europeans coming through here daily, I thought, aglow with their iconic achievement: They had Crossed the Sahara.

I had Crossed The Sahara. Not only that, I had *conquered*

the Sahara, the first person to achieve this feat in the manner in which I had done so. The significance of my outstanding personal achievement filled the bar and spread around the town like a faintly pleasant odour. Now people would see the mark of an extraordinary individual and give me respect, now they would take me seriously. Other pistes I had crossed may have been longer, sandier or harder to follow, but they hadn't *crossed* the Sahara. I had beaten the biggest desert in the world and I felt absolutely marvellous.

Nothing of the sort of course. I did feel marvellous, a marvellous relief that I had slipped through without too many problems and crossed the sands into another, more lively cultural sphere. It had been an eventful 48 hours: getting lost, the crashes, lost again and then catching fire. But at least I was learning to deal with events as they happened rather than react to them as malicious jabs of fate sent to make my life a misery.

Perhaps it's obvious that such "First person to..." epithets are simplistic media shorthands, dreamt up to titillate excitable book-buyers. But is there really anything to be impressed about in the feats themselves? Should one be awed by the recent self-mutilatory ventures of Ranulph Fiennes or Fiona Campbell. Is the battle against the truly awful hardships suffered in the name of exploration by the likes of Burton and Speke anything more than a battle against personal demons, a journey designed not to locate "the fountain head of that mighty stream [the Nile]" but rather to resolve some gnawing internal inadequacy? (The extraordinary Burton had a galaxy of other intriguing facets, of course).

Because of their exploits we can now celebrate in the knowledge that the Nile starts in a big lake close to some mountains; we are certain now that crossing Antarctica is bad for your health and that the streets of Timbuktu are not paved with gold. John Marriner dedicated his book *Sailing to Timbuktoo* to the irrefutable "courage and endurance" of, among others, Mungo Park, who struggled remorselessly through the lands of West Africa to what purpose? To ascertain the *direction of the flow* of the Niger River!

Surely these heroics must all be part of the same competitive urge, a quest for eminence and in the end, immortality. Less competitive cultures must regard such disingenuous quests with bemusement. To me the most memorable line from Michael Asher's *Impossible Journey* – the account of his gruelling camel trek across the width of the Sahara – was a comment by a dumbfounded Niger border guard to whom Asher outlined his pressing challenge: "What will you westerners think of next?"

Asher and his wife are exceptionally tough individuals, as are (or were) Fiennes, Campbell, Scott of the Pole, Burke and Wills and other long dead post-Columbian heroes of geography which history has credited in helping make the world a smaller place. But while it is amusing being the first, it's often nothing more than a combination of circumstance, hard work and luck.

Lautréamont, a nineteenth-century French writer had the right idea in this stirring tirade from his bile-drenched rant, *Les Chants de Maldoror*:

> The chemical peculiarities of the mysterious vulture that watches for the carcass of some dead illusion. Precocious and abortive experiences, obscurities with a flea-like shell. The terrible obsession with pride. The inoculation with deep stupors. Funeral orations, envies, betrayals, tyrannies, impieties, irritations, bitternesses, aggressive tirades, insanities, spleen, rational terrors, Strange misgivings the reader would rather not feel. Grimaces, neuroses, the cruel routes through which one forces last ditch logic. Exaggerations, lack of sincerity, the nuisances, platitudes, gloom, the dismal childbirth worse than murders...It is time at last to react against what offends us and so imperiously bows us down. You're being driven incessantly out of your mind and caught in the trap of shadows built with coarse skill by egotism and self esteem.

On trying to leave Arlit I was turned back at the first of countless roadblocks for want of the right stamps. Algeria may not have been a barrel of laughs, but its bureaucracy was a breeze compared to the Sahelian nations. At the second attempt, I learnt that I was now lacking a certain form and so back I went again to spend another day and a half getting a *laissez passer* and other paperwork.

I was looking forward to Agadez; indeed I'd been looking forward to it for several years now, ever since my first, aborted, desert venture. But the town, a more evocative, sub-Saharan version of Tamanrasset, failed to make an impression on me. What clothes had not burned got stolen while drying overnight in the irresistibly-named *Hotel Sahara*, and as dusk fell, squads of mosquitoes took flight from the flaking shower cubicle. Most guests seemed to belong to a jaded group of French mining engineers listening to a South African radio station. Ordering rashly from a mystifying menu one night, I was served a plateful of tinned Brussels sprouts in sprout sauce.

In fact I hadn't given Agadez a chance and if I'd just paused and explored for a few days instead of relentlessly moving on I might have learned and seen something, maybe even taken a camel up into the Aïr or the Ténéré.

This will to keep moving is a symptom of nervousness and fear. Sure, it's great to be here on the far side of the desert, but every passing day brings with it the possibility of something going Terribly Wrong: theft, breakdown, running out of money, who knows what? Best to get the whole risky business over with, develop the pictures and sit back safely knowing that you'd been there and done that. Alone on a bike, the feeling of relentless exposure is intense. There is an exhilarating feeling of freedom too, but the insecurity it brings drives you ever onward. The mentally unacclimatised desert traveller walks a tightrope, focused so intently on The Finish that he becomes oblivious to the interim.

Three days later I found myself slumped, cross-eyed with exhaustion on a sandy hill overlooking the Niger River. The

heavily patrolled tarmac highways of Niger were behind
me. I'd passed mud-hut villages – definitive African
imagery from childhood picture books and the better
Tarzan films – where women slung their millet pounders
upward with a clap, bringing them down into the mortars.
The spacious capital of Niamey was also behind me. Too
big to comprehend, I'd spent an awkward night in the
Grand Hotel and breakfasted like some vacationing mogul
on the terrace overlooking the river.

And now having ridden up the road that became a track
that became two parallel troughs of sand all the way to Gao,
I sagged against my bike, worn out with the effort of keeping the machine upright on a track which surely could not
have been negotiated by anything less than a tank.

Just before the Niger border at Labbezanga a boy had
rushed out from the riverside track shouting desperately

'*Popotome, popotome!*'

Was there an emergency, was his family drowning in an
upturned pirogue? Was it some kind of trick?

'*Popotome!*' he'd yelled in alarm, pointing towards the
river, but uncomprehending I'd ridden on, only later realising he was desperate to show me some hippos basking in
the river. I'd no time for hippos, I had a continent to cross,
and I'd already become hardened to Niger's roadside has-
sles and scams.

The crossing into Mali had been the same wily game of
palm greasing. Half a packet of powdery biscuits and a
map of the Ivory Coast (which I was now planning to miss)
had been enough, along with some bogus entry fee. I was
learning that border bribes were far from something as bla-
tant and crude as a cash payment, although these were
doubtless welcome too. It was just a way of life where a "little something" was the custom for all such dealings. Many
travellers boast that they never pay bribes on principle and
yet it is denying an established local practice which is part
of the economy.

Since that first venture south of the Sahara my few

bribes in West Africa have never amounted to more than some trivial but token gift which acknowledges the power of its enforcer to let you pass. Once understood and mastered (something I've never been there long enough to do), bribery enables the dramatic acceleration of Africa's grinding oficial transactions, and for civil servants (many of whom remain unpaid for months), mild extortion is built into their salary.

But for the moment I was in Mali with a one-week visa to get me the 1500 miles to Senegal. The sun was setting behind the hills lining the west bank of the Niger river below me and out of nowhere a young shepherd appeared to stare at me.

'*Très fatigué,*' I said simply. He stared silently at me for a bit with his hands tucked under his chin and then picked up his crook and walked off.

Down by the river the *hippopotames* were yawning and as the sun dipped below the horizon a thick chorus of frogs began croaking from the river. The brighter stars appeared and village fires sparked up along the far bank bringing with them the sound of beating drums which filled the fading twilight. I was too tired to cook or eat but the thought that I'd finally arrived in the Africa my father had once described was nourishment enough. Astonished that people still drummed in African villages, I imagined some age-old celebration being played out and woke up with the dawn where I lay.

A Blue Man

Breakfast in Gao's *Hotel Atlantide* was a simple affair served in the dusty foyer. Coffee, bread and jam. Though the place didn't quite evoke the ambience of faded colonial grandeur suggested by its name, I was glad to use it as a haven from the voracious local kids who baited bush-dulled visitors for sport. Expecting a straight answer from any of these grasping urchins was pointless. By trial and error I'd managed to locate the police station and the post office; the tranquil two-storey *Atlantide* wasn't so hard to find, but the ferry across the Niger still eluded me.

"Good day, do you know the way to the ferry please?"
"Take me on the back and I'll show you."
"There's no room, just point which way."
"It's hard to find without a guide."
"Just tell me the direction, how far?"
"Give me a hundred francs!"
"No. Which way?"
"Give me a present!"
"Piss off!!!"

These days Gao is little more than a dust-choked terminus at

the southern end of the thousand-mile Tanezrouft piste across the Sahara. Its location on a navigable stretch of the Niger waterway which loops anachronistically into the Sahara's southern underbelly has done little to enhance its commercial opportunities. The shrinking of the semi-arid Sahel in the face of the encroaching desert has for years been strangling the town's future and only the regular transit of motorised trans-Saharans has kept the town going.

All the harder then to imagine Gao as the thriving 100,000-strong capital of the Songhai Empire whose boundaries ran from present-day Senegal to Niger's Aïr Mountains and from what is now Nigeria to the salt mines beyond Taoudenni. It was the last of the three great West African medieval empires, following on from the smaller but equally influential kingdoms of Ghana and Mali.

Gao was founded in the late-fourteenth century by Sonni Ali Ber, a conquistadorial descendant of the Sonni dynasty with little time for the rigours of Islam. He set about retrieving territories which the Tuareg and Fula had grabbed from the fading Mali Empire, liberating the parallel city of Timbuktu 200 miles upriver and then moving south into the inland delta region to capture the important market town of Djenne and the Dogon lands of Bandiagara. It is said his military strength lay in his highly mobile riverine navy and at one point he even started digging a canal from Ras el Ma near Timbuktu to Oualata (in Mauritania) where more Tuareg dogged him.

After his death, Ali Ber's son kept a similarly short leash on religious influence but was eventually overthrown by Mohammed Torodo who founded the more devout Askia dynasty. (Torodo's small pyramidal tomb in Gao is the sole relic of that era.) With the approval of the powerful marabouts, the empire really hit form after Torodo was granted the caliphate of the entire Sudan. There followed a succession of short-lived Askia rulers right up to the mid-sixteenth century when the state reached its territorial zenith, feeding Europe with caravans of gold, slaves and ivory.

Then in 1591 the "Moroccans" arrived in force. Expelled from Andalucia and hungry for extra land in Africa, they set about extinguishing the last West African empire. Aided by firearms then unknown south of the Sahara, the sultan's army was able to capture the vast territories of the Songhai almost overnight. A chronicler of the time wrote: "Everything changed after the Moroccan conquest. It signalled the beginning of anarchy, theft, pillage and general disorganisation."

It's difficult to imagine a great empire dominating such a vast area just half a millennium ago. What commodities would there have been to banter and what would have been the value of a desert state? True, this part of the world was considerably less arid five hundred years ago; the Niger River flowed reliably all year and animal and mineral resources were much more prolific. And what is an empire after all, any empire, British, Roman or Songhai, but access and control; a network of far-flung mercenaries, tax collectors and loyal administrators.

After weeks riding through the desert the ferry trip across the Niger was over much too soon. I leant on the rail and let my eyes sink into the pea-green waters swirling past the bows. I would have happily tumbled in but for the well-worn admonition to stay well away from African waters where bilharzia flukes would tear you to shreds like a shoal of rabid piranhas.

It was a brief moment of calm in the pressing need to get across Mali in five and a half days. As far as I knew, a sealed road ran almost uninterrupted from the far bank to the capital, Bamako, over eight hundred miles away. From there the way to Senegal and Dakar was less clear. It was reportedly possible to put a vehicle on the train which linked Bamako with Dakar and the sea, but instinct told me that the expense and limitless bureaucratic possibilities in obtaining a ticket would probably make it a waste of time.

For the rest, and they were few, a notoriously rough piste spanned north towards Mauritania before dipping down to Kayes from where a track led to the seasonal Filingue River and Kidira in Senegal. Thereafter another famously undrivable piste led to Tambacounda where a road continued west to Dakar. It didn't occur to me that visas may have been easily extendable. All I could think was that by overstaying my time by even a few seconds the Malian authorities would have every excuse to sling me into some festering lock-up or charge me a huge fine. Paranoia at being in a strange land had shrivelled the optimism which brought me here in the first place.

The challenge of covering vast distances was a despatch riding mentality which has been hard to shake off. Speed meant safety and invulnerability; slowing down, hesitating, was extremely perilous. I felt I only had a certain capacity for dealing with the myriad new daily encounters: good ones like the river's curling waters, or bad ones like Gao's kids. And choosing a route out of Bamako was still a worry, one of many petty and tedious anxieties which dominated my day-to-day thoughts while travelling through West Africa. There is little doubt that the greater satisfaction of my travels is the thrill of planning and the rose-tinted reflections long after my return. Only then do you think...if only I'd slowed down a bit, explored that area a bit more and just stopped moving.

Not long after setting off down the highway for the long run to Bamako the bike veered off a bend and came to rest with a flat front tyre. As I rode over to a shady tree to start the repair a camel-borne Targui approached me, dismounted slowly and with some difficulty hobbled his stubborn beast. I'd never encountered one of the "blue men" – so-called because their indigo-dyed robes stain their skin – though I'd seen them strolling hand in hand down Tam's main drag, aloof and proud. I was as intrigued by their romance as anyone.

The nomad, a little chagrined by his camel's obstinacy, stood watching me grapple with my inner tube for a while. Here was a travelogue-worthy encounter between the traveller and the nomad whose mutual affinity bound them beyond simple words.

'*Salaam Aleikum*,' he said, offering the traditional Muslim greeting recognisable from Morocco to Sumatra.

'*Bonjour*,' I replied, too preoccupied and slow witted to use the correct response "Aleikum Salaam."

I was struggling to inflate the tube to which I'd already glued four patches; a legacy of the previous day's thorn thicket diversions when the track to Gao had become unrideable. I was now out of patches and nearly out of glue, but hopefully the next big town would replenish these essential items.

'*Tabac*,' said the Targui with his hand outstretched.

'*Je n'ai pas*,' I nodded, irritated by the still-hissing tube, the flies and now his ingenuous begging.

'*Thé?*'

'*Uh?*'

'*Thé? Donnez-moi. Sucre.*'

I was irritated by his lack of shame, his rudeness. Couldn't he see that now was not the right time to be asking me for handouts. And anyway, what did I have to give out of my denuded resources that would not wipe them out altogether? I offered him some of the dates I'd bought in Gao and which I was now avidly chomping my way through but, probably as sick of dates as only a desert dweller could be, he ignored them.

Where was the proud nomad beholden to no one but the wind and the stars? Disappointed by this encounter, I've since read that though they are disdainful of sedentary societies, nomadic cultures also see them as a source of commodities. In some Aboriginal languages the slang for "white man" is "meat" and this Targui saw me simply as a source of goodies if not to plunder (which was outlawed) then to scrounge from. In a city, slumped against a wall, such a beggar would have been commonplace but here out in the wilds where he was presumably living the unfettered life of his choice it upset my touristic sensibilities.

Eventually he wandered back to his grumbling camel and rode off, but for me it was a good lesson in appearances. Here, a picture postcard Targui dressed in the full regalia of his tribe and subject to all my romanticised prejudices had turned out to be nothing more than a guileless scrounger who appeared as equipped for his travels as I was.

A few years later I had a much more satisfying Tuareg encounter in the back streets of Bamako. I was cutting purposefully through the back blocks towards Niaréla, wondering where my short-cut would emerge, when from round a corner appeared a vision which brought me out of my self-absorption. Three Tuareg, tall and distinguished in their veils and long robes, sauntered along nonchalantly, lugging their camel saddles on their shoulders. A trio of cocky yokels from up-country come to see what the big city was all about, their casual pace betrayed a sneer at the squalid Babylon surrounding them. All nomadic tribes of the Sahara, but particularly the Tuareg, have a history of fierce antipathy to their sedentary neighbours, a mutual loathing fuelled by fear and contempt that has its roots in centuries of merciless slave trading and piracy on the caravans that traded West African riches with the Maghreb to the north.[*]

At the time of my visit the Tuareg, former warlords of the Sahara, were at it again, though this time the motive was political independence rather than commercial gain. Ransacking towns, besieging military outposts and robbing unlucky overlanders right down to their underpants, their

---

[*] The Bedouin of Arabia have a telling folk myth to explain the origin of all living things. According to the legend, the nomadic Bedu were fashioned by God from the wind, restless but free. The stay-at-home farmers, on the other hand, were the bi-product of donkey dung.

activities had led to the closure of the two main Saharan routes and the cutting off of northern Mali into a *zone securité*. The sight of these pitiless and proud *hommes bleus* was once again cause for wariness.

Seeing me looking at them, the nearest of the three grinned and dismissively flung me the customary toubabian appeal,

'Donnez moi cent francs.'

I shook my head, smiling and, indifferent to my rebuff, they strolled on languidly, revelling in their collective aura as the bad guys in town.

The Hills are Alive

The kilo of succulent dates I'd bought in Gao had gratified my sugar-starved taste buds but had had an even more relaxing effect on my shrunken innards. By the time I'd passed the looming volcanic monoliths of Hombori more contemporary eruptions were brewing in my bowels. Then, weakened by a self-imposed fast, I fell for the temptations of a roadside restaurant and tucked into some over-chillied slop served over a solid lump of rice. Within the hour I was back in the bushes again, paying the price for my culinary curiosity.

The temptations of Bamako's restaurants and hyper-expensive supermarkets delayed my recovery still further, though there was little else to keep me in the Malian capital, a frenzied overcrowded metropolis that was probably home to more people than the rest of Mali's major towns put together. Full of crumbling colonial relics, ugly Soviet-funded monuments and ancient Sudanese market halls – all of them surrounded by an ever expanding shantytown of rude dwellings – it was hardly the ideal haven for a weary traveller. Nonetheless I had a serviceable hideaway at the *Hotel Majestic*, a good enough place as any to perform my African hotel ritual: crank the fan up to "max" and flop on to the bed.

At the railway station, uncooperative staff did nothing to alleviate either my ignorance or my lethargy and defied all attempts at unravelling the secrets of the Dakar-bound train. Worn out by a day spent traversing the noisy, polluted streets to no effect whatsoever, I resolved to leave the city next day at dawn. With a mixture of adventurousness and direct route logic I decided to take a sinewy short cut directly across the Manding Highlands – the path of the railway – rather than the longer and reportedly arduous piste round to the north via Nioro. It was the last day of my visa and the likelihood of covering the 300 miles to the border across jungle tracks was slim, but I'd just have to face that bridge when I came to it. As a consolation, the idea of a back country track excited me, and the presence of the railway line could make this an easier route to navigate than the desolate northern piste.

In the humid light of dawn I quietly pushed my bike out of the Majestic's courtyard and on to the city's slowly stirring streets. From behind crenellated walls smoke from breakfast fires rose straight up in the motionless air. Knowing only that the way was north, I crossed the ocean-bound rails with a quick glare of resentment and rode up onto the hilly northern perimeter of the city where the president's palace spread out in secure seclusion.

I felt a thrill at the challenge of the unknown road ahead. According to the map, the track wriggled northwestwards, criss-crossing the railway which it was probably built to serve. In places it was even marked with the Michelin's reliable green band designating a "picturesque stretch of road." Big rivers drained northwards off the Guinean highlands while great sounding names like Bafoulabé, Ambidedi and Badoumbé rolled off the tongue with the rhythm of African drums. Better still, the piste wouldn't be as harsh as the desert. I was certainly in no state to cope with brutal exposure: pulling off the road to check the map on the capital's outskirts I simply fell over in a state of dozy frailty.

Half an hour from town a sign pointing west into the

bush indicated 180km to Kita, the only major town on the way to Kayes and the Senegalese border. I passed through villages where ragged, salty-faced children stared at the bike in wonder. Ruined colonial buildings loomed out of the undergrowth encircled by somnolent village compounds of mud and straw. Most of the way to Kita the railway was to my south so regaining my bearings on the many confusing branch pistes was simply a matter of heading resolutely south until I hit the rails. Nevertheless, disorientated by the myriad tracks, short-cuts and diversions around the larger villages I soon found myself circling through light jungle, riding up hills to search for clues or squeezing between huts into a village to ask the way *"Chemin de fer? Chemin de fer s'il vous plaît?"*

Then the track ended at a rubble-strewn river bed even the bike could not manage. Though it was surely not the main track, a rail bridge spanned the creek and, taking a chance that the twice-daily train was not due, I rode up the embankment and bounced along the sleepers. Unable to ride down the steep bank on the far side, I dragged the bike to the bottom on its side just as the clatter and rumble of the *Océan-Niger* Express passed overhead. Humbled by my close encounter, I decided that it would be ear-to-the-track, Indian-style on any subsequent bridges.

By late afternoon I finally reached the sprawling regional capital of Kita, birthplace of many of Mali's fabulous caste of *jalis*. Funded by local noblemen to literally sing their praises, the jali or *griot* caste are the custodians of Mali's traditional songs (many of which have found their way onto the CDs of the World Music scene). This region boasts some of the finest voices and most uplifting music of West Africa, if not the whole continent. That the sound of what became known in the Twenties as The Blues was being played here for centuries before is now well known. Carried in the memories and traditions of black slaves, the distinctive influence of West African music on the sounds of North and South America is unmistakable.

Unrecognised to the West until only recently, it is the continent's richest traditional heritage, as complex, refined and influential as the architecture of Asia. As the title of one of the Malian musician Ali Farka Touré's albums suggests, it is The Source.

Pressed for time and knowing it would be simpler to sleep in the bush than attempt to find a hotel in Kita, I rode on into the dusk, making the most of the good clear piste before falling asleep by the track side. A subsequent photo showed me sunken-cheeked and grey faced, perhaps more ill than I realised but happy to be unknown and on the move.

By the middle of the next morning I was staring at the piste which ended abruptly at a muddy bank where the Bakoye and Bafing rivers met. Presumably it continued out of Bafoulabé, half a mile away on the far bank where what I took to be a ferry carried traffic across. Figuring that the ferryman would waft over when he was ready, I parked the bike conspicuously by the mooring posts and sat back, pleased at an excuse for a rest. A young girl came to wash her clothes in the river, indifferent to my presence, but later when her mother grumbled unintelligibly at my asking about the ferry, I began calculating the chances of loading the bike onto a pirogue or two to get across. Was this was why everyone took the train or the Nioro piste?

In fact it was just another of the many foolish assumptions I was making on this first venture south of the Sahara. In the desert there is a finite limit of options: either the piste continued or it stopped and you went back. Either it was rideable or you avoided it. But here in the lightly wooded jungles of western Mali, flooded by seasonal downpours and speckled with innumerable villages, countless variables confounded decisiveness while the lack of danger dulled my wits: what did it matter if I got lost down here, I was bound to find something or someone eventually.

Sure now that this was no ferry mooring, I looked

around from the higher banks of the broad confluence for a clue. Seeing nothing but fishermen dividing the waters in their dugouts, I rode upstream to find a village and a little later came upon a long box girder bridge which, obvious to all but me, spanned the banks.

Planks lying across the sleepers suggested motor vehicles shared the bridge and one or two pedestrians plodded across with their shopping. Still wary of meeting an oncoming train or somehow getting into trouble, I hesitated by the bridgehead mulling over the wisdom of my actions. Then, summoning up the nerve, I set off across the bridge, eyes fixed ahead for the blunt nose of the train and ears awaiting a yell of reproach from some rail official. None came, and safely on the far side I stumbled around the edges of Bafoulabé before finally locating the westbound piste which led on to Kayes.

For days Malians had been shouting something unintelligible at me as I zipped through their villages and now at last I worked out what it was. They were yelling *"Rallye! Rallye! Rallye!"*, mistaking me for a front runner of that year's Paris–Dakar Rally, which was building up like a tidal wave a few days behind me. In fact I was desperately trying to keep ahead of the race, knowing that prices would soar and commodities vanish as soon as the first riders roared into view.

Accustoming myself to the pleasures of my back track excursion through Mali, I stopped off at the rather depleted waterfall, the Chutes de Gouina, and took an exploratory bite from some bitter-tasting fruit which grew by the track side. The washed-out, stony piste climbed and fell through the rocky hills and a wild pig charged out from the high grass across my front wheel. As the afternoon wore on an old road sign, sponsored long ago by "Essence Sphinx", warned rather redundantly of bends ahead, as similar signs in Algeria had exhorted "Sable!!" – sand.

That evening, lost again on a fissured limestone plateau

on the outskirts of Kayes, I finally found my way into town along the conventional route. Acknowledging more cries of *Rallye!! Rallye!!* and buying an expensive half-tank of petrol, I attempted to make a run for the frontier post at Diboli with my nearly expired visa now beginning to curl at the edges. A little over a hundred kilometres – a couple of hours – but in the end, worn out by the long day, I collapsed in a copse of portly baobabs near the halfway point at Ambidedi. Whatever censure lay ahead for me at Diboli, I'd done my best; surely the guards would be sympathetic to the vagaries of a newcomer on the Kita piste.

But there was worse to come. Running briskly along the sandy track through the trees next morning, a cruelly angled rock finished off *both* inner tubes in one go. Having used up the last of my glue and patches the previous day, it was time to test out the Sahara Handbook's innovative tip and stuff the irreparable flat tyres full of foliage, clothing and anything that came to hand. With no clothes left other than those I was wearing, I packed the tyres out as advised and, thinking myself to be a wily bushmaster, rode on in a floppy meander to Diboli. Within a couple of miles the grass was reduced to useless powder and I oscillated along at 15mph until the bemused villagers of Diboli surrounded me, trying to make sense of my urgent enquiries. Desperate to get a straight answer for once and more than happy to pay for it, I pulled out a bag of rice and planted it in the nearest man's hand, asking:

'*Où est la frontière? – Diboli?*'

'*Diboli?*'

'*Oui la frontière à Senegal?*'

'*Là bas,*' he pointed down to the shallow river.

'*Merci beaucoup,*' I said gratefully, charged with the urgency of getting to Diboli as soon as possible so that whatever fine I might collect would be reasonable.

'*T'as crevé,*' he said, pointing to my flat tyres.

'*Oui, je sais,*' and I wobbled off down the river bank and over the stream. Thinking the town I was approaching was

Mali's frontier, Diboli, I rode up to the policeman snoozing in his hut and with my passport planted the last of my *cadeaux* on him, an unopened pot of jam I'd bought in Bamako.

'*Merci,*' he said with a generous smile, '*bienvenu à Senegal.*'

'Senegal?'

In my rush to avoid the death sentence which Mali issued to foreigners who overstayed their visas by a day, I'd raced out of Diboli, somehow managing to bypass the frontier post, and crossed the Filingue River into Senegal. Relieved at my lucky break, I spent the rest of the day waiting for the westbound train to take me and my bike to Tambacounda, where the advance guard of the Rally were already strutting around in sponsored boiler suits and clipboards. At Tamba's station an American biker who'd ridden this far from the Arctic Circle gave me a spare back tyre to replace my now ruined item, and an overnight bus trip to Dakar saw me back in Tamba' with new inner tubes.

Dakar's *Hotel du Marché*, a charming brothel, was my home for the few days it took to sort out some money and a vessel to Spain. The thought of driving all the way back across the Sahara to Algeria was unbearable and, after so many adventures, seemed to be asking for still more trouble. Berths on the freighter were twice the price of a flight and so, wonderful though it would have been to sail back to Europe with my bike, I flew to Madrid and picked it up at Valencia docks.

Walking to the port one of my shoes finally separated from its sole. I shrugged at another small swipe of bad luck, and yet within a few paces I came across a rather snazzy pair of suede Chelsea boots just lying there on the dockside. Slipping them on, this lucky find seemed a fitting metaphor for my recent travels: with a Zen-like indifference to misfortunes large and small, things always worked out all right in the end.

Christmas Dinner at the Bar Mandela

B ack in Mali about eight years later, I found myself in
Kayes once more, this time celebrating Christmas
Eve with a bowl of rice and peanut sauce. Things
had lightened up a great deal in the intervening years as
Mali had begun to distance itself from Soviet political influence, and travel was no longer the continual headache of
permits and battles against ridiculously short visas that it
had been. With a planned visit to Guinea extinguished by
pre-election border closures, I decided to spice things up by
seeing what would happen if I went south to a place called
Kénieba in a remote southwestern corner of Mali, close to
the Guinean and Senegalese borders. I was hoping that
once there some kind of local transport would lead over the
border to Kedougou in southeastern Senegal – if no such
service existed I could return to Kayes and take the train
west like everybody else.

'*Bonsoir*, is there a lorry to
Kénieba?' I asked a man eating next to me.
'Yes, there are many *camions
russes* going to Kénieba, ask
at the *citerne*.'
'*Merci*.'
Why red lorries I thought,
maybe it's some kind of slang
for the local service? I set off
in search of the "citerne"
which I imagined to be a
tanker – was it a tanker
which took passengers down

to Kénieba, clinging to the hatches and hoses?

'*Bonsoir, où est la citerne?*' I asked various people.

'*Là bas,*' they all replied confidently as I searched a side road for some tanker-like entity.

'*Citerne?*'

'*Oui, là.*'

'*Merci.*' And so it went on until I wandered up a wide road and asked three boys sitting by an old petrol pump.

'*Soir*, do you know where the "citerne" is?'

'*Oui*, this is the citerne.'

'Oh, I'm looking for a lorry to Kénieba,' I added, glancing around for a lorry park or even a red lorry.

'*Ah, Les Russes.*'

'U-hm.' I nodded in polite incomprehension. Most of my French exchanges were sustained with this technique which helped span the frequent conversational crevasses.

'*Tu vas à Kénieba, t'es un Russe?*' I nodded dutifully, only half understanding the question. "Russe" could also be the local slang for *toubab*. After all, the Tiwi Islanders off northern Australia used to call white men *murantani* "red faced one who sweats a lot" – an apt description for most European visitors to Africa too.

From that point on the evening was given over to an all-out search for Les Russes, with me perched on the sandwich rack of Hamadou's Mobylette and having only a vague idea of what was happening. Knees hooked over my ears, we bounced purposefully around the town's nether regions, stopping off at small shops, strangers' houses and street corners to shake hands, pass the time of evening and ask after *Les Russes*.

'*Un camion Russe part demain matin à Kénieba*'. That much Hamadou had discovered, but the identity of the driver, and the departure point, were still unknown. I was intrigued and a little confounded at this cat-and-mouse game around Kayes' back streets. If it all came to nothing as I expected, then I'd just carry on into Senegal by rail.

When Hamadou led me through a string of bars I began to wonder if he wasn't merely enjoying the attention of whizzing a *toubab* around town in front of all his mates. We popped into the al fresco disco bar opposite the *Hotel du Rail* where we seemed to do nothing more than walk hand-in-hand across the floor (me, unused to this custom, rigid as a plank), pause for effect and then walk back. While there I noticed a tanker parked in the grounds emblazoned with a white star and the words "petrol" stencilled on the side in Russian. *Russe.* Russian! Was this the "red lorry" I'd been hearing about all evening, maybe even a *Russian* lorry?

Next morning I was indeed coughing up the requisite fee to Alexei and his two cohorts for the hundred-mile drive down to Kénieba in the back of his chunky Vostok diesel. Having spent the night with Hamadou's family, I thanked him for his tireless assistance with a tip and clambered in the back to join the other passengers sprawled over sacks of grain and drums of oil.

For years I'd been looking forward to one day riding this scenic stretch of road, passing along the base of the serpentine Falaise de Tambaoura, but all I was to see for the next four hours were the backs of the three silent Russians and the small section of track just in front of the cab. The other passengers were similarly mute, opening their mouths only to inform me that my jacket was slowly soaking up some leaking paraffin. If the Russians were Christians, they appeared to be keeping control over their Christmas Day celebrations. I myself always like to spend this day in unfestive places if at all possible and the back of a Russian lorry in west Mali certainly beat extended family gatherings around the dinner table.

'*Est ce-qu'il ya un camion à Kedougou?*' Same routine, different place.

I stood outside Kénieba's sole garage at the top of its one main road which lead to its small market.

'*Peut-être demain*,' I was told by a mechanic tangled in the entrails of a Land Rover, a thankless task with which I was only too familiar.

'*D'accord, je reviens demain*,' I replied, presuming the cross-border jaunt to Senegal was a daily affair. I walked down the town's deserted main road, shaded to the east by the tawny cliffs of the Tambaoura escarpment. As I passed by, children turned to me shouting "*Russe! Russe!*" and even "*Bonne Fête Monsieur Russe*" rather than the more customary chant of "*tou-bab, tou-ba-bou*." This curious cultural anomaly was eventually explained to me, but for now I entered the darkened cavity of the *Bar Mandela*, Kénieba's sole source for the commodities of alcohol, gossip and sex.

The bar was under the temporary management of Aga, an independent-minded young woman from Ghana bearing the twin cheek scars of an Ashante, who was minding the place while her sister was away visiting. Being Ghanian Aga spoke English far better than my bush French and, hearing of my plans to catch a ride into Senegal, she offered to ask around, saying 'Someone always goin' somewhere from eya.'

In the courtyard of the Mandela compound half a dozen women from teen- to middle-age pottered about, hanging up clothes or plaiting each other's hair. Ignoring their mutterings and giggles, Aga showed me to my room, pointing out the shower, toilets and a huge well on the way. The room appeared to be already occupied by a person of very few possessions, the most conspicuous of which were an illustrated Christian Scientist Bible and a huge stack of condoms. As she left Aga urged me to make sure I locked my door from the *inside* at night.

Crossing the yard again later, I studiously avoided the gaze of the bar's permanent residents, especially the pretty young one. I'd made that mistake once before at the *Hotel du Marché* in Dakar when an innocent smile across the breakfast table had resulted in a categorically unwanted hard sell in my room half an hour later.

Aga returned from the market with my lunch, dropping a hunk of fish, an onion and a yam into my lap along with my change. There didn't seem much left – like anywhere in the world, remote places are expensive places.

'Der's a pan, wota ova der, chacol ova der,' she said curtly as I stared blankly at the uncooked ingredients. Weeks of street food had shrivelled my culinary imagination and I fumbled with the small charcoal stove I'd spotted everywhere but never actually used. And what did one do with a yam or a fish's torso? Away from a Teflon and Sabatier environment, I was temporarily flummoxed into half-baked inactivity. Seeing my typically useless male confusion at the sight of a pot and pan, Aga, took over.

'Give me da knife and pudat ova der. Don't you cook for yaself where you live, or does mama do et ol?'

Aga was clearly an emancipated woman fed up with Africa's venal, lazy and stupid patriarchy. Her directness amused me and she never stooped to the half-resentful queries about the imaginary Good Life I led back in Europe as others tended to do.

With a few deft movements my fish was filleted, the yams peeled and set to boiling merrily. Minutes later the simple Christmas dinner was ready. As I ate, a jeep pulled up outside and a pale, sweaty European walked into the bar, peering around in the gloom.

'*Pivo*?' asked Aga, cracking open a beer bottle.

'*Ah, bon*,' he nodded.

With a combination of my Russian and his English, he explained that he was an incoming engineer for the Russian gold mining outfit, heading out to their site near the Guinea border. Moping his brow and glancing furtively around the bar with restrained unease, he didn't seem to be relishing the prospect of his assignment. Meanwhile the jeep's tanned, burly driver, evidently a seasoned visitor to the Mandela, strode in, slapped some money on the counter and opened the huge fridge, grabbing a beer for now and a crate for the road.

'*Davai*,' he said to the engineer, tossing his already empty bottle into a bucket. '*Idjemy*.' Let's go.

So these were the fabled gold fields of West Africa from which the legendary prosperity of Timbuktu had grown and which were now being picked clean by Soviet technology. For at least two thousand years caravans had crossed the Sahara from Morocco, adding salt to their burdens at Teghazza in far northern Mali to trade with the shy, gold mining "Senegalese". This exchange took the form of a "silent trade" with the beating of drums presaging the tendering of goods by the visitors. Responding to this signal the troglodyte miners would first inspect the offerings, especially the valuable salt, and then return, setting their treasure alongside. The traders would inspect the quantity of gold and either take it or withdraw unsatisfied, but once a deal had been reached the drums would roll again and the caravan would return north. The source of the gold always remained a mystery. Once a miner was captured but died without revealing its location. All that was known was that the place was called Ouangara – until it was discovered that the word *ouangara* meant "place where gold is mined."

The trade flourished with the fortunes of the Ghana Empire at the beginning of this millennium and the imperial capital of Koumbi Saleh (now a few denuded stumps in southern Mauritania) grew to become one of the greatest markets in Africa, a trans-cultural entrepôt as pivotal as the Silk Route caravanserais of Central Asia. (These too prospered in the same era, where Roman merchants had also traded silently with their Chinese counterparts.)

Aga explained how in olden times the women had gone out to pan the bush for gold for their husbands who would hoard the precious crumbs: the greater a man's reputed stash the greater his status. Like a scrooge he didn't do anything with the treasure, didn't convert it into useful commodities. Instead he hid the hoard until he died. Some townsfolk still boasted of several kilos of gold hidden out in the bush – a ploy whose feckless conservatism irritated the hard working Aga.

'Da people eya a so schupit. Dey eat da sem food evry day an' live in one room, and out unda a rock dey hide a big bag of gold. Schupit! One day I find me one-a dem bags and I outa here! An' now da govamen leda Roshans dig eet op an' tek eet away. You tink dey pay Mali? Pah! dey show a leetbit, but most of it go out in dei back pocket to Senegal.'

And that wasn't the only clandestine commerce that went on in Kénieba. Every Tuesday a lorry drove up to Guinea's mountain border at Kali to load up with cheap beer and cigarettes; what official presence there was in town was easily looked after. To me it all seemed rather exciting: face to face with a thriving frontier economy making ends meet any way it could.

At the garage next day the mechanic was stretched out in the same position across the Land Rover's engine and had the same answer; maybe tomorrow. Someone else who'd heard about my need offered to run me over to Kedougou straight away; a hundred mile journey at a pound a mile. Not being a border-skipping Russian miner with a can full of gold and diamonds, I decided to give it another day, though I began to doubt the chances of the Rover being repaired and suddenly filling up with Kedougou-bound passengers. Maybe I'd have to truck it back to Kayes and catch the train after all. Walking back down the road to the Mandela, kids looked at me shyly with their hand at their mouths and then, just after I passed summoned up the courage to blurt with a giggle:

'*Monsieur Russe! Davai! Davai cadeau!*'

'*Davai! davai! davai!*' ("come on, give") the bolder ones yelled.

That night in the bar all was quiet as Aga and I chatted away. She'd mentioned my Senegalese transport predicament to Diallo, a mechanic down at the market who owned a *"grand moto"*. He'd come over later to talk money. What was it I wondered, a BMW or a salvaged Rally racer? Knowing that he held the cards as far as the price went, I fixed a figure in my head which I was prepared to pay and waited. There were no lights in the bar or indeed anywhere else in Kénieba. Instead a flickering candle dribbled itself over its predecessor, flashing our shadows around the gloomy room. Another *"camion Russe"* pulled up outside and the driver hopped out.

'*Pivo, davai,*' he said impatiently, glancing at me.

'*Zdrastvitie.*'

'*Zdrastvitie,*' I replied, already getting perilously close to my limit of Russian.

'Are you from the mine?'

'*Niet,* tourist.'

'Tourist? he said incredulously. *Rosyanin?*'

'*Niet, ja budyet Anglichanin.*'

'Ah, "How iz zi kween?"'

'*Ochin harasho.*' (Very well.)

'*Harasho,*' he replied, draining his bottle in one gulp and turning to Aga.

'*Vodka?*'

She shook her head as if she'd been asked this question a hundred times already '*Demain,* tomorrow, er…YUTRO VODKA, YUTRO SOIR'.

'*Arrr,* bother,' (or somesuch) he grumbled. '*Davai piwo encore,*' he demanded, this time showing six fingers. Walking over to the fridge she pulled out half a dozen chilled bottles which he stuffed inside his pockets and under his arms.

'*Svydanya tourist,*' he nodded, and walked out to the rumbling lorry.

'Deez Rushans dey drink ol da time. Drink, drink, drink ol da time. Den dey crash dey truck an dey dead, dead, dead – fo eva! Fo' die olredi las monf. Hit a tri an ol die. Is time fo a new candal.'

After a while a young man walked into the bar and, greeting me politely, began talking with Aga in Malinke, the regional language. Like most West Africans he had a working knowledge of at least three African tongues, as well as French, possibly some English and Arabic and here, maybe even some Russian. From what I'd seen the expatriate miners had little ability or inclination to learn even a few words of French.

His awkward fidgeting and glances out back made it clear that he'd come to the Mandela for more than just a chinwag and a beer, but Aga teased him with chit-chat for a little longer before sending him round to where the girls were sat by the well, swishing at mozzies.

Between Aga and myself nothing was said or acknowledged. It was an odd situation though somehow I felt it was right to keep up the pretence – or I was too embarrassed to pry. Fifteen minutes later the man wafted back to the bar on a cloud of euphoria, beaming, refreshed and relaxed. His transformation was quite remarkable, making the event less sordid than I'd imagined. The pretty one who I'd been obliquely eyeing up myself walked him to the door, also smiling, and for a moment I thought they might even kiss each other goodbye.

Outside, the blare of an unsilenced motorbike grew louder and then stopped outside the bar as the engine cut out with a final "BANG!".

'Ah, Diallo is hiya,' said Aga.

Next morning I bade goodbye to Aga and the Bar Mandela, planted 35,000 CFA (around £30) in Diallo's palm and perched on the back of his "*grand moto*" – a measly Honda 125 but as big as they get in Mali. I was looking forward to this, riding along the smugglers' tracks to Senegal; who knows were we might end up? We rode up the main street to the sound of a few bleating "*davais*" and then turned off onto a narrow path. Again I was leaving Mali without checking out, but by now I realised what was the point?

They'd hardly chase after you and it saved at least half a page in passport stamps.

Diallo rode expertly through the bushes, swapping from rut to rut and warning me to duck under branches while my hands clamped the rack or occasionally his steadying shoulder. On the steepest banks or in soft sand he pushed the bike along while I soon gave up any attempt at memorising the route for another time. Within an hour we stopped at a tiny village close to the Falemé River where Diallo lit up a cigarette, passed on some news and delivered a letter. Out here toubabery is unknown and what villagers there were just stared at the bike and me without a word.

The river was too deep and stony to ride through so we pushed the bike across with a dead engine and at the far bank tipped it up to drain the water from the exhaust. Then off we went again, along wider tracks and now officially in Senegal. By this time my numb backside had reached the far shores of catatonia and I was glad of the fag-and-engine-cooling breaks Diallo was having to take as the pace and the day warmed up. He spoke of taking his mechanics' skills to France and I told him of my motorbike travels in West Africa at which he seemed unimpressed.

Within an hour or two the road widened and became sealed and presently we arrived at Kedougou, close to Senegal's Niokolo Koba national park where French holiday makers come to hunt and observe the remaining wildlife. With a handshake and a small gift, Diallo turned about and headed home and I set off along an avenue of mango trees to see what I could find.

Battle of the Saharans

S teve and I were not getting on. Things had unexpectedly turned sour back at Assekrem, not even a week
out of Algiers, when a dark mood had enveloped him
after I'd eaten a piece of bread between meals. We camped
at the same God-forsaken patch where Helmut and I had
spent the night five years earlier but, after making a terse
comment about my infractory snack, Steve had made dinner and gone to bed early. I sat outside by the dwindling
fire until the last possible minute and then, judging the
atmosphere to be marginally less icy in the van, crawled
into the back as quietly as possible.

In Tamanrasset next day things had come to a head
when the washing-up bowl I'd left on the roof rack to dry
had got blown off on the way to a restaurant in town. A
spoon had also gone missing. Steve was keeping a tight
reign on the fury.

'Look, I'll buy you a new washing-up bowl at the market; I've seen plenty there.'

'They're not the same.'

'Well it's better than nothing.'

'They're not the same,' he brooded.

To be fair he had a point. Algerian Tupperware didn't have
the refinement and attention to detail of its European counterparts, but functionally they were hard to distinguish.
When you're moving on every day it takes a while to get
into a rhythm and on all my trips I'd lost small items
through absentmindedness. Steve claimed he'd never lost a
thing.

Then he did an alarming thing. He reached into the back
of the Land Cruiser for his secret stash of Scotch, unscrewed
the top and knocked back a mouthful. Though he admitted

to being fond of a pint, this act belied a rage that was disturbing. Something was dreadfully wrong and though I didn't know what it was, my carelessness had set it off.

For both of us this was *the* desert trip, a trip that we'd each been privately planning for years. When travelling together with SMT the previous year, we'd quickly established a shared passion for exploring the Sahara and had set about organising the Big One together, each with his own 4x4. Though I'd been keen to head for the Ténéré, we'd settled on keeping off the tarmac wherever possible and decided to head down to the Mauritanian Sahara and Guinea's mountain jungles.

Unfortunately for me that particular *annus* had climaxed with a *horribilis* end when my standard Land Rover (with which I'd replaced the temperamental 101) had blown up in Sussex one night. I'd only just recovered from a fairly major bike smash up too so, having done my best to keep my head above the excrement into which I'd been sinking lately, I accepted that this was not to be my year and the Big Trip would have to wait. In Switzerland Steve sympathised with my bad luck but offered me his desert-ready bike to make up a two-vehicle outfit. He would carry all the gear in his Toyota while the bike could be towed and when necessary I could enjoy the novelty of riding an unencumbered bike in the desert.

It was a generous offer but I was still nervous about my newly plated shin following May's crash and anyway after six desert trips I'd had it with bikes. I'd been dearly looking forward to the greater security and comfort of a 4WD, but it was difficult to turn him down if for no other reason than his own trip would be compromised into a solo venture. On the understanding that we'd share the driving I accepted his offer and after a bit of to-ing and fro-ing across Europe we'd set off for Algeria in early January.

Now in Tamanrasset something was seriously bugging him – surely not just my illicit nibbling or the missing spoon. Though we were never likely to be close friends, I valued Steve's experience and apparent level-headedness: both valuable qualities for a companion in the remote Sahara. Despite his rather inhibited and serious nature we'd got on well enough and were mutually excited about the unknown places which lay ahead.

Next morning he drove off without saying anything and returned hours later to tell me the trip was off and we were going back just as soon as Caroline could fly down in about a week. Fait accompli.

Steve's sudden change of plan had stunned me. Here he was with one of the best equipped 4WDs in the desert and he was going back because things weren't the same without Caroline in her own Toyota. I'd certainly been made to feel rather redundant up till then. Whatever I tightened, checked or locked was checked again and minutely improved upon – a trait of control freakery to which I was prone myself but something I expected to diminish as my usefulness was accepted. Perhaps he was under more stress than I'd imagined. After all I was riding his bike alongside his car and materially he had everything to loose. Steve delighted in his car's crafty mechanical modifications, all executed with a fastidious attention to detail; he didn't share my rather casual notion that a Saharan vehicle should be a basic, functional but ultimately disposable hack.

'If the trip's over then I think I'll head straight back. I'm not really happy about riding a bike anyway.'

'Oh? Don't you want to wait until Caroline turns up? We could do some pistes in the Hoggar, maybe the outer loop?'

'No, I've done those pistes, I'd rather go back tomorrow, save my money and do it properly next year in a car.'

I didn't imagine it would make any difference to Steve if I was around or not and, if anything, I thought he wanted to be rid of me. The last thing I wanted to do was tag along with the two of them around Algeria on the way home. But, hard though it was for me to believe, the mere thought of waiting for Caroline alone for a week made him change his mind and the Big Trip was back on. He went off to call Caroline again, suggesting she meet him in Dakar in a few weeks, while I marvelled at his astonishing fickleness. We agreed that Algeria had been annoyingly cold, the pace too fast and that I felt nervous on the bike. And from now on we'd share the driving or tow the bike wherever possible as originally planned.

His mood brightened while mine became suspicious. Grateful though I was to be here on his bike, Steve's peculiar flightiness made me look at him differently now. Abandoning the trip without consulting me was acceptable: if he genuinely didn't feel good about it, turning back was the right thing to do. But to change his mind again on such a feeble pretext? I'd go with him across the Sahara but if things didn't work out after that I'd head off on my own.

We retraced the piste to Bordj Moktar which we'd traversed together the previous year and then headed down the Tanezrouft into Mali where the weather warmed up appreciably. The sudden change made me feel lethargic and now I moaned about being too hot. The pace warmed up too and back aboard the bike I gave up trying to keep up with the speeding Toyota, cringing at the thought of coming off onto my left leg. The southern Tanezrouft may not be the Hanging Gardens of Babylon but why the 100kph rush? I put it down to the get-there-before-anything-happens nervousness I'd known myself alone on a bike.

The only time I'd experienced truly searing Saharan heat was late one September, a sobering lesson in the desert's enervating power. Temperatures were reaching 30°C by 9 o'clock, climbing up to 45°C by noon and staying at that level for three or four hours. I found myself sealing off my cuffs to wrap up *against* the skin-burning 45°C gusts. Now I really understood the adage "like driving into an oven."

Water became an even more critical issue than usual: what had lasted me three days in winter with plenty to spare was being guzzled away in twelve hours. Riding a bike at 50mph actually made matters worse. Dehydration was accentuated in this furnace blast and it was uncomfortable to ride for more than thirty minutes, no matter how keen I might have been to press on, before a drink stop became imperative. I could feel the dryness slowly creeping down my gullet and into my very core. At night I'd wake up rasping, my mouth and tongue about to solidify. At a vapourless 45°C the body just can't sweat quickly enough to keep itself cool; without water and shade, death would be certain in 48 hours.

In *Wind, Sand and Stars*, de Saint-Exupéry describes a touching scene (probably made up) that took place while he was stationed in the Western Sahara in the 1920s. At that time the Moors, in particular the refractory Reguibat tribe, were still a danger to French interests. The best thing crashed pilots could hope for if captured by the nomads ("...In those days our planes frequently fell apart in mid-air...") was to be sold into slavery or better still, ransomed back to the French. In an attempt to cultivate good relationships with the Moors, the French decided to take three of them to France, hoping to shame the men's fierce pride and arrogant belief in their indomitability. But Paris meant nothing to the three transplanted Moors, being merely a "very big" place where, unbelievably, no one carried a rifle. Only once in the Alps, taken to visit a huge thundering waterfall, were the Moors utterly transfixed. They stared in awe at the wondrous deluge and tasted the sweet water which no saline muddy well in their homeland could match. When their guide suggested they move on they begged to stay a little longer for, as the author recalls,

> "... the flow of a single second would have resuscitated whole caravans that, mad with thirst, had pressed on into the eternity of salt lakes and mirages."
> "'That is all there is to see,' the guide had said. 'Come.'

'We must wait.'
'For what?'
'The end.'"
They were waiting for the moment when God
would grow weary of his madness. They knew him
to be quick to repent, knew he was miserly.
'But that water has been running for a thousand
years!'"'

Back on our own battlefield Steve seemed engaged in his
own Paris–Dakar and, to my amazement, was to confess
that his prime enjoyment of desert trips was the trouble-
free verification of his vehicle and all its canny mods. Our
all-piste route from El Golea to Tam had included a technically complex crossing of some dunes near Gara
Khanfoussa on the way to Ain El Hadjadj where, in 1881,
Flatters had received his Tuareg warning and Pobéguin
ended up cannibalised by his comrades. For both of us the
dune crossing had been a test: we carefully read the tones
of the sands and reconnoitred with the bike before picking
a firm path through the trackless sands with the car. On
reaching a well on the far side of the erg we'd been amazed
to come across an eccentric German couple in a ratty
Beetle. Amazed that a forty-year old car had made it
through the dunes, Steve admitted their presence had
merely soured his achievement. While such "greater-
explorer-than-thou" envy is not uncommon among
Saharans, I admired the unconventional though able VW,
which made the gizmo-packed Land Cruiser look distinctly excessive.

The evening after we left Timbuktu (fuel, check in, quick
beer and then OFF!) I decided that tearing around after the
Toyota was not my idea of the ultimate desert trip. In a way
I was experiencing the powerless, follow-the-leader futility
of one of the SMT bikers and I didn't enjoy it at all. We'd
just wasted an exhausting hour shoving the mired Toyota
off a trackside dune which Steve had insisted on conquer-

ing just to prove that he could. To me such bull-headed machismo was the worst aspect of men in big cars and something no level-headed Saharan would contemplate. There'd be plenty of shovelling in Mauritania without looking for it.

'I think I'll head off when we get to Ségou [the next major town]. I'm not really enjoying all this riding around after you. I want to go off and do my own thing.'

I was determined to salvage my trip for my own ends. The shared driving had not materialised, the pace was ridiculous (we'd done around 2500 miles in less than two weeks) and everything I did was either wrong or inadequate. I didn't see such a separation as a failure, it was merely the right thing to do if I was not to end up feeling resentful. Steve was surprised and angry, not least because me leaving would mean he'd have to tow the bike around with him, blocking access to the back doors and making reversing (essential on the piste) impossible.

Though my mind was set, in begrudging appeasement he offered to let me drive the car, and next morning made a fuss of riding the bike, dressing in fully-protective waxed cottons, a full water bottle and a large bag of tools packed on the rack.

'Are you sure you need all those?' I asked. I'd not carried tools on the bike, figuring they'd be safer in the car which would always be close by.

'Best to be safe. I like to be prepared,' he replied tersely, pulling on some thick gloves.

We set off down a deep sandy track towards Niafounké (Ali Farka Touré's home town). After an initial tumble Steve was soon out of sight while I struggled to keep the wallowing Toyota in a straight line and moving through the soft sand. This was hardly a solution and in the present circumstances there was little doubt that our Saharan compatibility had expired. At the convergence of roads and tracks that marked Niafounké there was no sign of Steve and, unsure of the way, I decided to circle around town until I spotted the black bike. Suddenly there was an almighty thump on the side of the van and Steve's livid face glared at me through the driver's window.

'Why didn't you fucking stop for me back there! You could see I was stuck under the bike!'

'What are you talking about?'

'You know what I fucking mean, you saw me back there on the dune and you deliberately drove straight past!'

Steve had been doing some more trackside practice while waiting for me to catch up and had fallen over, ending up stuck under the bike. With my hands full of steering wheel and gear levers I'd not noticed this, but he'd thought I was making my point that "see: bikes *are* a handful" and driven blithely past. This assumption that I would ignore him, possibly injured, out of sheer spite stupefied me into a rare reaction of indignation.

'Are you crazy? Do you think I would just leave you lying in the sand? You must be out of your fucking head! What are we travelling together for if not to help each other. I'd never have passed you or anyone.' I was shocked that things had got to such a state that Steve really believed I'd leave him by the trackside. He realised he might have got the wrong end of the stick.

'Well I'm sorry, I really thought you'd seen me and driven on.'

Now our expeditionary relationship had definitely reached an irreparable nadir. If he was capable of making such alarming deductions then how would he react in a genuinely stressful situation in the desert? Absorbed in our own churning thoughts, we found the right way out of Niafounké on to the fast wide tracks which criss-crossed the mud-baked lagoons laid bare by the Niger river's seasonal floods. Up ahead Steve was riding fast, trailing a thin wisp of dust, when suddenly his back wheel locked up in a plume of grit and he wrestled the skidding machine to a halt. Today was not his day. Some tools had come loose and fallen into the back wheel's spokes, jamming the wheel instantly – he'd done well not to fall off straight away – and he was now stunned by another setback on the bike. My comment that morning didn't help quell his fury, but luckily only one spoke was bent. We drove on across the mud flat to find some shade for lunch.

'WHOA! STOP!, you're scratching the paintwork!' he said, thumping on the back of the van as I reversed it right under the meagre shade of a thorny acacia. Another small dig at my general incompetence, but soon I'd be off; just another couple of days, I thought. More than ever my help in preparing the lunch was rejected and so I squatted like a bad child by the trunk and waited for my share.

Obviously by demanding that Steve ride the bike, something in which he had little interest and now I thought about it, little experience, I'd brought all the morning's bad events to pass. If only I'd just quietly accepted my role as motorcycle outrider behind the pace setting Toyota there'd be no problem. But I'd had my share of desert biking over the last decade: for me there was nothing left to do on bikes, on which I no longer felt secure.

We sat down at the table.

'It's not working is it,' said Steve.

'No,' I replied

And we equitably went over the reasons why not. He was unhappy about me driving his pride and joy, I was unhappy about tearing across Africa and spending most of the time on the bike. And although I didn't say so, Steve's overreactions to the small and fairly commonplace setbacks, as well as his general my-car-versus-the-desert attitude, made me wish I'd never come. Though we were both avid Saharans, our attitudes to the desert were radically different. So much so that we could no longer bear travelling together, even though we'd enjoyed many of the experiences we'd so far shared.

The problem wasn't so much a clash of personalities,

more of wills. I'd immediately liked Steve's quiet strength and single-minded adventurous spirit when we'd first met that cold morning on the Tassili. Subsequent meetings through the year had done little to dispel that impression. With his mechanical background, his Land Cruiser was as safe and well-equipped as any car need be for the desert. But that orderly attention to detail seemed to be his over-riding interest, whereas for me the machine was just a means to an end. After many years I'd learned enough about vehicle preparation to make me fairly easy-going about that side of things. Impressive but ultimately futile piste-bashing was all very well but I wanted to rise above the preoccupations of the journey and feel that I was really there. And on this trip I thought that would happen.

At that point under the thorn tree I yearned to be free to set off by myself and have my own adventures. Steve spoke of a café owner in San or Ségou who he'd met last time he was in Mali. How about if he left the bike there and we went up to Mauritania to do the Tichit piste and then head for the coast. He could then pick the bike up with Caroline on the way back from Dakar. Though I was as curious to see Mauritania as he, surely that would be the place where his two vehicles were essential. And anyway I'd made my mind up to split at Ségou.

But when it came to taking the low road to Ségou or the high road to Néma in Mauritania Steve, unwilling to stash his bike with a stranger, proposed one final offer. We'd tow the bike or share the riding right across the Tichit piste fifty-fifty, though in tricky terrain it would be best with him at the wheel. On this clear proviso I accepted and we so turned north for Nara and the border to Néma in Mauritania's southeast corner where the 500-mile Tichit piste beckoned two Saharans battling to get their own way.

The Princess of Tidjikja

"...he leans towards his brother, whispers, and
stares at me.
'What's he saying?' I ask once again.
'That he will shoot you if he meets you outside the
fort.'
'Why?'
'He says you have aeroplanes and the wireless; you
have Bonnafous [a daring French officer]; but you
have not the Truth.'
Motionless in the sculptured folds of his blue cloak,
Mouyan [a Moorish warlord] had judged me.
'He says you eat greens like the goat and pork like
the pigs. Your wives are shameless and show their
faces – he has seen them. He says you never pray.
He says, what good are your aeroplanes and wire-
less and Bonnafous if you do not possess the Truth?'

Antoine de Saint-Exupéry
Wind, Sand and Stars

My bag sat in the dirt while I watched Steve, the
Toyota and the unwanted bike disappear into
the dust of the Mauritanian outback. No sooner
had he gone then a throng of commoting kids surged
towards me. A little
nervous at the fuss my
presence was causing, I
reached down to pick
up my bag and find
somewhere to hide. Is
there a hotel in town? I
asked the nearest boys.

'Take him to the
governor!' they cried,
'Take him to the gover-

nor!' the horde repeated, and like a scaled-down Gulliver I
let myself be carried across Tidjikja's main square towards
the boredom-slumped soldier who guarded the Governor's
residence. Slapping his rifle, he shoo-ed away the kids and
grumpily bade me sit in his gatehouse and wait. At last
things were about to get interesting.

We'd done the Tichit piste, an ancient trade route which fol-
lows a string of wells dotted along the base of the like-
named escarpment which divides the rolling dunes of the
Aoukar basin from the rolling dunes of El Djouf
(Hassaniya[*] for Empty Quarter). Sure enough I'd ended up
riding the bike all the way: before we even left Mali Steve
had insisted on driving after I'd grounded the car on a
hump and apparently jeopardised the clutch.

   In Néma we'd hooked up with a venerable local guide
known as Nani. A Gandhi lookalike with a mischievous
glint in his eye, Nani's enigmatic lifestyle appeared to make
him something of a local hero; every time a new batch of
adventuresome tourists rolled into town Nani would disappear with them and their fabulous vehicles, only to
return days later, still with pocketfuls of dosh. That glint,
along with Nani's professed lack of French and other curious habits were to irk Steve once it became clear that guiding us to Tidjikja was a handy opportunity for him to catch
up with his nomadic chums still living along the piste.
Actually there wasn't even a piste: most of the way to
Tidjikja, where the governor now waited to judge me, had
been entirely trackless. We'd seen only one vehicle along
the entire stretch, a stripped-out ex-Rally Range Rover
inhabited by a family of nomads who'd wordlessly offered
us a bowl of *zrig* (sugared camel milk).

   The route had turned out to be less dramatic than we'd
imagined. Vegetation was relatively prolific, giving the
region a drab, Sahelian appearance, and a stiff wind had

[*] Mauritania's principal native language, a form of archaic Arabic.

misted the clear horizons we'd anticipated. At the semi-abandoned ruins of Oualata, just north of Néma, I'd expressed an interest in stopping for a couple of days to get the feel of the historic place.

'I couldn't imagine anything worse than staying here for two days,' Steve had said with a grin that suggested he was seeing the funny side of our consistently disparate expectations. He prided himself on his ab-so-lute self-sufficiency and hated sleeping near towns let alone in hotels while in the desert.

Oualata was one of a handful of still-occupied medieval citadels which thrived during the Almoravid dynasty (better known as the Moors whose decline only set in once they were expelled from Andalucia in 1492 – the year Columbus set sight on the New World). More than the fabled Timbuktu in Mali or Chinguetti on the far side of the Djouf, Oualata remains celebrated as an unrivalled centre of Koranic scholarship and students still come here to memorise tenets of Islam inscribed on aged wooden tablets. Even today the school has a waiting list ten years long to fill the twenty available places.

While waiting for Nani, who'd disappeared on arrival, we wandered up the side of the hill into the town's crumbling old quarter: narrow alleys of collapsing arches, time-worn steps carved into the rock and stout wooden doors decorated with bronze and copper. Behind some of these portals we glimpsed secluded courtyards where families went about their day and where you could just make out bits of local bas-relief ornamentation indigenous to the Tagant province of Mauritania. Not surprisingly we towed a wake of curious kids who settled with us around the car once our walkabout was complete, gabbling, giggling and pilfering bungees behind our back.

The bright smile of one of the girls reminded me of the description of the Nemadi dog-hunters in Bruce Chatwin's *The Songlines* which I was reading at the time. The Nemadi are an all-but-extinct nomadic group and, according to Chatwin, their women are famed for their beauty and legendary smiles. What is the secret of your smile, the author had asked one woman. "Meat!" came the unequivocal reply.

Cast even lower than the black Harratin slaves who serve the typically haughty Moors, the Nemadi are accused of an assortment of blasphemous acts, not least of which is the eating of the porcine wild hog along with the similarly endangered antelope. When antelope hunting was outlawed by the Moorish government in the late Sixties, the Nemadi lifestyle was itself endangered and they have now been virtually marginalised out of existence.

Mauritanian society is rigidly hierarchic with the aristocratic *Hassanes* at the top followed by the pious *Tolba* caste of holy men. Below this are the silversmiths, the shopkeepers, the *Zenaga* pastoralists and the *Abid* or *Harratin* (freed black slaves) and finally, though virtually insignificant, the untouchable Nemadi. Those of the upper echelons are all *bidan* (white) Moors of Arabic descent while the lower castes are of mixed blood or of the indigenous tribes of West Africa.

Up till the end of the Sixties the majority of Mauritanians of all castes were nomads, but then severe droughts and the subsequent intervention of overseas aid drove the wanderers into the shanty towns (*bidonvilles*) on the outskirts of Nouakchott. With the nomadic lifestyle still a first-hand memory for most of the sedentary population, modern Mauritanian society is a society learning how to cope with urbanisation, a society that's collectively coming out of the desert. It's tempting to bemoan this drift towards a more urban culture for, as Chatwin points out, the nomadic way is the original, authentic human way of life, an existence that is motivated by an instinctive impulse to keep moving and a disinterest in excessive material wealth. According to his alluringly romantic analysis of early human history, the nomadic era represented humanity's

Golden Age when Man lived in harmony with Nature, respecting if not worshipping it as his treasured resource and taking from it only what he needed.

Civilisation (in this context, the sendentarisation of humanity) brought about Man's downfall through the subjugation and control of both Nature and the majority of humans by powerful if unqualified oligarchies. With civilisation came the suppression of our urge to wander. To repeat Chatwin's clever Biblical allegory, humankind has sacrificed the unaspiring contentment of Abel the shepherd for the insatiable greed of Cain the farmer. For nomads, the hoarding of briefly prolific foodstuffs to combat seasonal shortfall is unknown, instead the people move *with* the seasons; nomadism is systematic and not aimless wandering as many assume. Progress or, as they see it, change, is anathema to true nomadic peoples who strive for nothing more than the freedom to live their lives just as they have always done.

Very few of today's nomadic peoples retain a "pre-civilisation" lifestyle in which, tellingly, organised religion plays a minor role. Most, especially the Arabic tribes who lived close to civilisation's origins, and particularly the Moors, have adopted the concepts of hierarchy and status which were introduced in Sumeria. Only some Aboriginal groups of Australia's Western deserts and, in Chatwin's view, the ever-smiling Nemadi, preserve a carefree simplicity untroubled by inequality and respecting simply experience, age and a good day's hunting.

In the days out of Oualata, we passed huge camel herds being watered at wells along the base of the cliff, the only landmark for our guide to follow. At Tichit, another former Almoravid citadel once renowned for its glass beads which were traded as far afield as Venice and Scandinavia, Steve was forced to give a soldier a lift to Tidjikja, a service which he performed with increasing resentment as the conscript offered his tips on how to drive through the dunes that were slowly engulfing Tichit and its palmerie. Every so often Nani would get out and jog ahead of the car for twenty minutes at a time, looking for the firmest ground and occasionally advising us to double back and try another way. He'd return to the car not even out of breath and nibble on a few peanuts. On our last morning together I joined him for a hunk of camel meat and a glass of mint tea expertly boiled on a few twigs. When I finally managed to gnaw off a rubbery chunk, it proved to taste worse than the sandloaf Chadli had cooked at the Cathedral the previous year.

Arriving in Tidjikja, I sold my crash helmet to the delighted *gendarme*. This time Steve didn't even try to persuade me to stay and he drove off sullenly towards Nouakchott. I was out of the race.

For three hours I sat obediently in the gatehouse until at sundown I was summoned into the house. I had no intention of causing a nuisance to anybody in town and, although I wasn't sure what I was doing next, I'd been expecting to sleep out in the dunes until something worked out. Now I foresaw an impatient and busy governor demanding why this scruffy *nsarani* (Hassaniya's version of toubab, which derives from "Nazarene"; Christian infidel) had been brought before him when he had a province to run.

Inside, I was directed to some cushions in an otherwise bare, lantern-lit room and there I sat with the governor's family, who seemed delighted at the opportunity for some light-hearted bantering with the novel *Christophe*. But they pulled themselves together respectfully when the governor swished fleetingly into the room, swathed in the ubiquitous sky-blue robes of a Moor; he shook my hand and then swished off again to a funeral in Atar.

In all my desert travels I'd never got anything like as close to communing meaningfully with the locals as I did in Tidjikja. I was thrilled and intrigued by my unexpected good fortune, but I was also plagued with an unbearable self-consciousness and a nagging anxiety over transgressing the presumably strict Islamic mores of my aristocratic hosts. And now, with the presumably strict cat away, the mice – mother, five sons and six daughters – were able to play, and for a couple of days I was their amusing piece of cheese.

The Lord of the Tagant's family lived in isolated splendour, separated from the commoners' slums in the main part of town by a sandy oued. Their home looked as if it had once been the former French colonial governor's residence, a terraced quadrangle around a spacious courtyard set around a well. Nearby outbuildings and barracks also kept their chins above the encroaching sand and housed the lowly staff and a variety of redundant Land Rovers. When I first saw their accommodation I presumed they must be as poverty-stricken as the people in other parts of Mauritania that I'd seen. But in fact the caste-topping Hassani family (those who carry this noble name count themselves among the Prophet's direct descendants) was as wealthy as any surviving aristocratic clan. The daughters wore lustrous jewellery, £100 slippers from the rue St Pantoufle and Pierre Cardin jumpers.

Yet despite these fancy trappings they stayed true to their nomadic roots and lived in the villa as if it were a huge tent. The electricity had never been used and light fittings hung from the walls like dead birds. Doors, shutters and windows were left broken where they'd fallen and there was no furniture, not even a table. Wood was so scare here that it had all long since been burned or put to better use. Instead, the bare room where we ate was simply decorated with carpets and cushions on which all reclined with ease, while the servants ferried in Moroccan silverware laden with cous cous and finger bowls.

As a guest I was treated more as an honorary Moor rather than a *nsarani* and so everything was done for me – laundry, meals and the arrangement of my flight to the capital – by a loyal retinue of black servants. Mauritania is perhaps best known in the West as that vile country which only a few years ago was finally compelled to outlaw slavery by a right-thinking UN, but these Harratin were a close and influential part of the extended family who nonetheless did all the disagreeable labour which no true Moor would sully their hands with. It's a good thing I was so spoiled, as the only time I emerged from the sanctuary of the villa and ventured across the oued, I got stoned by the town's brats.

From the first day Nadjat, the coquettish and spoilt seventeen-year-old, had flirted eagerly for my attention to the irritation of other more eligible suitors also staying there. All six daughters were plump, well-rounded *sminas*, "fatties", and thereby culturally very desirable. Brainwashed by tales of severe Islamic lore as regards to women, I was perplexed by her cheekiness and reckless smiles. I reacted modestly, dreading committing some gross taboo.

'Christophe, *pourquoi n'as tu pas de femme? Tout homme a besoin d'une femme,*' she'd bleat. '*Christophe, aimes tu les femmes Mauritaniennes*?

'*Er, oui, ils – elles sont très jolies.*' At which she'd cover her mouth in a spray of giggles.

Invited to breakfast one morning in Nadjat's and her sister's bedroom, the radio announced that Nelson Mandela was to be released from prison. She reacted indifferently to the news and instead asked pleadingly whether I had any books I could give her as she was keen to improve her English. The only book I had with me was my not quite finished copy of *The Songlines*. I pointed out the many references it had to Mauritania, including the Nemadi who, if they survived at all, did so under her father's jurisdiction. "*Ils sont sales*" she scowled at the mention of the scummy dog hunters, but she accepted the gift which to me seemed fitting.

On my last night there, a feast of yet more infernal cous cous was prepared outside for an Egyptian doctor from the local hospital. Most of the evening passed in formal banter, with me hypocritically swallowing an unresolved atheism to feign regular Sunday morning excursions to church: to a devout Muslim, belief in any monotheistic religion is far more acceptable than no belief at all. As the topic continued on this tricky subject, Nadjat's two younger brothers took an excited interest and dashed in to get their Koran. They flicked through the pages of illuminated Arabic script to point out references of the Nazarene to me, and with a touching fervour, fingers tracing the words, quietly sang the holy verses together. In the end, they implied, to become a true Christian I had to convert to Islam.

The evening relaxed a little after the doctor bade his farewells. Everyone slid back further on their cushions and Nadjat's provocative joking with me went a little too far:

'Christophe, je t'aime! Christophe demande moi en mariage!'

'That's enough, Nadjat,' one of her older sisters reproached shortly and she sank back to fiddle with her veil. Back in Britain a few months later, I happened to be sitting on a bus, hurriedly reading a book called *Travels in Mauritania* before motion sickness caught up with me. Its intrepid author Peter Hudson had just camelled down to Tidjikja from Chinguetti and, invited to lodge at the governor's residence as custom required, fondly described a flirtatious ingenue by the name of "Nanja" who he met there.

> She had the sort of beauty men fight wars over, pure and unblemished. Her laugh was as light as a forest stream, her eyes as moving as jewels, and she teased me with unabashed cruelty…"Which one of us is the most beautiful? [one of the sisters would ask]…is it Nanja…It must be Nanja, she wants to marry him."

> …She would watch me smoke and say things to me that I did not understand, but *'Hejala''* was a word I knew and one she often used. It meant 'to marry'. She would ask if she could fill my pipe for me…'See, she is his wife already, [the others] would say. She fills his pipe for him.'

So, I thought with a smile, she toyed with all the *nsarani* boys who came to town!

The morning following the feast I was driven to the airstrip to catch the twice-weekly flight to Nouakchott on the coast. Accompanying me was Tidjikja's sole permanent *nsarani*, a self-confessed definitive example of a "do-gooding" Peace Corps Volunteer by the name of Patrick, stationed here to instruct a women's weaving co-op in the ways of modern market practices. It was a thankless task for him, alone out in this desert outpost, his efforts stifled by anti-American suspicion and barely tolerated by the governor and his family. Getting to know his colleagues later in Nouakchott, I was struck with a deep admiration for what they admitted were largely futile efforts in changing entrenched Moorish habits. After Sudan, the Republic was considered one of the hardest three-year postings a PCV could get and all admitted that they learned much more from their experience than their "needy" hosts. To me their unenviable lifestyle and grass roots activities were much more laudable than the a/c apartments and booze-laden diplomatic bags of USAID and the like.

We bundled into the family's last running Land Rover, Nadjat inviting me to squeeze into the slender gap between her thigh and the door. I squirmed in with polite decorum; surely such familiarity was inappropriate? Only later in Nouakchott did I realise that, as long as a Mauritanian woman kept her hair veiled, she could behave with a lack of reserve which Saudi Arabia – one of this poor country's principal benefactors on condition it follow certain Islamic codes – would have found horrifying.

At the airport a soldier tipped out my bag to the amusement of all onlookers. Half the town had lined up to meet the incoming plane but the three sisters who'd come to see me off kept their distance from the crowd. As I walked to the plane my last sight of them was the comely threesome sat on the dirt runway, their pristine silk robes fluttering in the breeze. I looked over my shoulder and as if by design, the three princesses tilted their heads simultaneously, smiled and waved goodbye.

Acknowledgements

Thanks to all the following organisations and writers for permission to quote extracts of their work:

Arabian Sands by Wilfred Thesiger Reproduced by permission of Curtis Brown Ltd, London on behalf of Sir Wilfred Thesiger. Copyright © Wilfred Thesiger 1959.

Wind, Sand and Stars by Antoine de Saint--Exupéry, translated by Lewis Galantière, published by Pan in association with Heinemann © 1987.

Sahara Handbook by Simon and Jan Glen, published by Roger Lascelles © 1987.

The Fearful Void by Geoffrey Moorhouse, first published by Hodder and Stoughton © 1974.

Sailing to Timbuktoo by John Marriner, published by William Kimber © 1973.

Sahara by Emile Gautier, English edition published by Hippocrene Books Inc, New York © 1987.

The Rough Guide to Morocco, 4th edition, by Mark Ellingham, Shaun McVeigh and Don Grisbrook, published by Rough Guides © 1994.

"Everybody's Talkin'" written and composed by Fred Neil © 1967 Coconut Grove Music, Co., a division of Third Story Music, Co. Inc. California, USA. Lyric reproduction by kind permission of Carlin Music Corporation, UK Administrator. Used by permission. All rights reserved.

Maldoror and the Complete Works: Lautréamont. Translation © Alexis Lykiard (Exact Change, 1994).

Travels in Mauritania by Peter Hudson, published by Flamingo © 1991.

DESERT BIKING
A Guide to Independent Motorcycling in the Sahara
by Chris Scott

Draw from the author's fifteen years experience in the desert and recently revised and updated, *Desert Biking* is the only handbook of its kind in English and is pertinent to adventurous off-road bike touring anywhere in the world.

Subjects covered include:

- Selecting and preparing a suitable machine.
- Advice on what to take and how to carry it.
- Guidance on riding techniques in sand and on rock.
- An expanded section on GPS satellite navigation aids.
- Latest details on the trans-Saharan route via Mauritania.
- A selection of eventful biking tales from the Sahara.

This fully-illustrated book also elaborates on Saharan climate, geology and wildlife, water, health and essential documentation as well as describing a number of detailed itineraries in the Sahara with accompanying maps and reviewing over forty books relevant to the subject.

For extracts and news of all Travellers' Bookshop publications type "Desert Biking" in the Net Search box. Alternatively, our web site address is:

http://www.shapero.com/rarebooks/

The Travellers' Bookshop
(Bernard J. Shapero Rare Books)
32 St. George Street,
London W1R 0EA

0171 493 0876 ~ Fax 0171 229 7860
e-mail: rarebooks@shapero.com